THE THOUGHTFUL GUIDE TO FAITH

Tony Windross

BOOKS

Winchester, UK
New York, USA

Copyright © 2004 O Books
Reprinted 2005

O Books is an imprint of John Hunt Publishing Ltd.,
The Bothy, Deershot Lodge, Park Lane, Ropley, Hants, SO24 0BE, UK
office@johnhunt-publishing.com
www.o-books.net

Distribution in;
UK
Orca Book Services
orders@orcabookservices.co.uk
Tel: 01202 665432 Fax: 01202 666219 Int. code (44)

USA AND CANADA
NBN
custserv@nbnbooks.com
Tel: 1 800 462 6420 Fax: 1 800 338 4550

AUSTRALIA
Brumby Books
sales@brumbybooks.com
Tel: 61 3 9761 5535 Fax: 61 3 9761 7095

NEW ZEALAND
Peaceful Living
books@peaceful-living.co.nz
Tel: 64 7 57 18105 Fax: 64 7 57 18513

SINGAPORE
STP
davidbuckland@tlp.com.sg
Tel: 65 6276 Fax: 65 6276 7119

SOUTH AFRICA
Alternative Books
altbook@global.co.za
Tel: 27 011 792 7730 Fax: 27 011 972 7787

Text: © 2004 Tony Windross

Design: Cover: Infograf, London
Text: Graham Whiteman Design, Halifax, Canada

ISBN 1 903816 68 8

A CIP catalogue record for this book is available from the British Library.

Printed in Singapore by Tien Wah Press (Pte) Ltd

THE THOUGHTFUL GUIDE TO FAITH

Tony Windross

CONTENTS

ACKNOWLEDGEMENTS

My personal faith journey has been long and eventful, and I have benefited from conversations with very many people. I would like to thank my parents for getting the whole thing going when they enrolled me in the church choir at a tender age. I would also like to thank the Reverend Peter Shepherd, for his unwillingness to leave me in a state of dogmatic unbelief, and for his friendship over many years. The Reverend Andrew Piper and the Right Reverend Nicholas Reade each gave generous support in different ways and over a long period. Of seminal importance at a very critical time was the encouragement of the Right Reverend Peter Ball: without him things would have turned out very differently.

Appreciation is also due to those members of the congregations in Eastbourne, East Grinstead and Sheringham who have shared my ambition of trying to find ways in which Christianity might stand some slight chance of engaging with the contemporary world. My family is at the centre of everything that I do, and Peter, David, Andrew and Paul are a constant source of joy and surprise. The debt I owe to Pat, my soul mate and very best friend is beyond all words, which is why this book is dedicated to her.

PREFACE

It's difficult being a liberal, especially a *radical* liberal. You *want* to be tolerant of everyone and everything, you *want* to respect their right to say things that seem completely bizarre, you really do. The problem is that some of the things that other Christians say are actually dangerous, in the sense that they are likely to put people off Christianity altogether. If religious outsiders keep hearing what sounds like one stupid claim after another, made by people who obviously take Christianity very seriously, then it's hardly surprising if they decide they don't want anything to do with *any* of it!

There comes a point when it is no longer possible simply to sit quietly, biting both lip and tongue in a desperate attempt not to hurt or offend anyone. Unless liberals are prepared to stand up and get shot at, the future for intelligent Christianity is bleak. It's not about wanting to create a liberal hegemony, but about wanting to ensure that a true diversity of voices is heard, so there is at least a possibility that interested outsiders may find someone who speaks to them on whatever is their particular wavelength. At present the dominant voices that are heard coming from the Church are those on the Evangelical wing, and there is no doubt that what they have to offer is what many people want. Evangelical churches often attract large congregations, and far from decrying their success I am happy to applaud it. But I also want to see the survival of churches with dignified liturgies, fine organ music and intelligent preaching, because there are many people for whom the Evangelical style of worship and thinking is both alien and impossible.

This book was born out of frustration and embarrassment. The church where I serve as vicar is used for many baptisms, weddings and funerals, huge numbers of concerts and other community events, and is also visited by lots of holidaymakers. This means that a high proportion of the people who come through its doors are not part of our Sunday congregation, or indeed *any* Sunday congregation.

It *frustrated* me that when they came in, there was nothing of a religious nature for them to browse through that tried to address, in an intelligent way, the reasons why the majority of people in our society want nothing to do with the Church. And it *embarrassed* me that no such material seemed to exist *anywhere*, with 'introductions to faith' invariably depending on one's ability to believe six impossible things before breakfast. I resolved to do something about this, and the result was a series of six short leaflets, each asking a different question such as 'Why bother to think about God?' These were deliberately sharp and provocative, not because of any wish to upset, but in the hope that they might grab the attention of the casual browser. They were not intended for those members of the congregation who felt completely at home in the Church, but for those who were on the edge of faith, either just inside or just outside, and who were wondering whether the Church actually had anything to offer them.

Demand for the leaflets has been high, and there have been many positive responses, together, of course, with some negative ones. The latter have invariably come from people who were not part of the target audience, and who *are* able to accept the teaching of the Church in the form in which it is traditionally presented. They were outraged at what they saw as a diminution of the Christian message, but relatively unconcerned that ever fewer people find this message of any interest whatsoever.

I am much more ambitious for Christianity than they seem to be, and want to explore whether (and if so, how) it can be presented in ways which engage with intelligently sceptical people where they actually are. Because this tends to be a very long way from where most members of the Church are, it means that trying to address their concerns and doubts in a positive way is bound to upset those who, for the life of them, really cannot see what the problem *is* with Christianity. But understand it or not, unless they are able and willing to support such an attempt, there is every reason to suppose that within a couple of decades the Church in this country will have lost even the slight toehold that it currently has in people's lives. The Gospel is currently being proclaimed in what amounts to a foreign language, and if the Church is not willing to translate it into something that makes sense to people, it will have to bear a grave responsibility.

Picture the scene at the World Cup Final. The stadium is full of people, from dozens of different nationalities; everyone's watching the match, but each group is speaking in their own language. They don't understand what the others are saying, but assume that it's similar to what they themselves are saying. Each is looking at the same events but responding in their own way. It would be absurd to claim that unless the Japanese spectators spoke in English their understanding of the match would be in some way inadequate – but this is what many of those inside the churches say with regard to the relationship between religion and life. Their view is that unless others use the same sort of words as they do (and indeed use them in the same sort of *way* as they do) no correct understanding of life is possible.

Those outside the Church tend to speak a completely different language to the insiders, who themselves communicate in a variety of dialects, some of which are so broad that other Church insiders have such difficulty understanding them that they wonder whether the same language is being used. Unless the different groups within the Church are able to find ways of respecting and tolerating each other, the Church is bound to disintegrate. And unless interpreters are found who can do something about the linguistic divide between the Church and secular society, the Church is bound to fade away.

Because Christianity is now very much a minority taste in our society, we need to begin from a position where it is seen, in effect, as guilty until proved innocent. This means a starting point of either atheism, agnosticism, or, in an increasing number of cases, sheer indifference. The underlying assumption is that unless and until good grounds can be given for taking faith seriously, most people in our society will continue to live their lives without any reference to Christianity, which will continue in its rapid downhill spiral. To take it seriously, people need a reason, indeed probably lots of reasons. The form of this book reflects this, and tries to address the many very good objections that people have to Christianity. It's easy to ask why bother with *any* of it, but that's such a large, unmanageable question that I try to break it down into lots of individual issues, which are inevitably connected in all sorts of ways. The chapters are self-contained, and can be read in any order. Inevitably there is some overlap between them, but this has been kept to a minimum through the use of cross-references. I have tried to use inclusive language, but sometimes, especially with regard to personal pronouns about God, I have used the masculine form; this is simply for convenience and no ontological implications are intended.

As with the original leaflets, the book comes with a health warning: *it is not intended for those of a nervous disposition, or those who are easily shocked!* Rather, it is for those who, as members of the faith community or as interested onlookers, are depressed and mystified by much of what goes on in the name of Christianity. It is unashamedly informal, and much more a conversation than a seminar. In no way scholarly or exhaustive, there are no footnotes or references, and it deals only cursorily with topics that each merit at least a book rather than a brief chapter. The brevity of the chapters should help to make them more useful as a basis for discussion groups than if they were exhaustive – and exhausting!

I take seriously the objections that are raised by religious outsiders, and suggest a number of ways that they might be able to understand those elements of Christianity that seem particularly problematic. My underlying assumption is that Christianity must be accessible to everyone – and that includes the sceptics. They have spiritual needs, and at present simply gag on the fare that is offered them by the Church. Doubters are valuable members of society, and must be made to feel welcome in the Church as well. Unless Christianity is capable of coping with the challenges and objections that they bring, it is probably not worth bothering with. I have no time for the religious equivalent of political correctness, and raise all sorts of questions that are often left unasked. However, there is no wish to be either wilfully provocative or gratuitously offensive, but simply to encourage debate, and show that, despite almost overwhelming evidence to the contrary, all sorts of perspectives *are* welcome, and you don't *have* to put your brain on hold to take religion seriously.

Chapter 1

THINKING ABOUT GOD

Most normal people have no interest whatsoever in religion, and that's because they've got no interest in God. If someone doing a survey asked them whether they believed in God, many would probably say that they did – but there would be few if any differences in their lives compared to those who were bold enough to *deny* the existence of God. For almost everyone in our society the subject of God is completely and utterly irrelevant, and in many ways this is an enormous pity.

The most basic question, of course, is 'Does God exist?' Are there any reasonable grounds for thinking that he/she/it *might* exist? If so, is there anything to suggest what he/she/it might be like? Although these are potentially the most important questions that anyone can ask, they generally *don't* get asked. And this is largely because so many of the claims made by Christians are so odd and so open to ridicule that most thinking people simply shake their heads and walk away! Are they wrong to do this? Is religion in general, and the question of God in particular, simply a throwback? How can *any* of us decide which ideas are worth bothering with and which aren't? There's so much religious nonsense around that we need a filtering mechanism to help us sort it all out – a bit like the judging panels for awards such as the Booker Prize that point us in the direction of those books which are most likely to be worth reading.

Only a philistine would dismiss the very idea of religion out of hand: so many people find it worthwhile that to see them all as stupid would be terribly arrogant. And although truth can never be established on the basis of a show of hands, there comes a point when the number of hands raised is so great that at the very least it should give us pause for thought. The great world religions constitute an obvious short list of potentially reasonable beliefs, but even this is far too long. The only practical solution for most of us is to focus on the religion that is dominant in our own culture; and although we live in a multi-faith society, the main religion in Britain is clearly Christianity. So when faced with the phenomenon of Christianity, what is the casual outsider to make of it?

Most people would say that belief in God is at the heart of Christianity: if you *can* manage to believe in God then Christianity is a possibility for you; if you *can't*, it isn't. And although that's a bit hard on those who would like to be part of the Church but can't manage the belief bit, most religious insiders wouldn't see the problem. *They* can believe, so surely everyone could, if they really tried? (There's almost an implication that people's lack of belief is due to either stupidity or wilfulness). And this is where it usually all stops: with those *inside* and those *outside*.

The problem for many outsiders is that God is often talked about in terms that appear to be ridiculous. He (and it's usually a 'he') is understood as a sort of invisible super-person, who made everything, and who now keeps an eye on it all. Sometimes he's thought of as having a body, sometimes he's thought of without a body. Sometimes he's thought of as living in a particular place, (heaven), sometimes he's thought of as being all around us, and sometimes he's thought of as both at the same time. The whole idea begins to creak quite a lot as soon as it's looked at for more than a couple of minutes, which is presumably why it usually isn't. Not surprisingly, many intelligent, thoughtful people refuse to have anything to do with any of this, mainly on the grounds that there is no evidence worth speaking of to support it. Their reaction is perfectly reasonable, and raises the question whether this actually is what Christianity is all about.

The God at the heart of much Christianity is often used as a sort of explanation-of-last-resort, a God-of-the-gaps. But inevitably, as the ability of human beings to explain things gets ever greater, the need to wheel him in diminishes; and the current position seems to leave little for him to do apart from start the universe off, perhaps via the 'Big Bang'. Sometimes Christians find it comforting to hear scientists say that they are unable to explain 'how it all started', and conclude that such admissions show that Christianity was right all along! But perhaps this is because such questions can *never* have an answer. And if people try and use religion to give an answer (e.g. 'God made everything') all that may be happening is that one unknown is being replaced by another.

The heart of the God-problem for many people is the ontological status of God, traditionally thought of as *a being* of some sort. If we think along those lines then he/she/it must presumably 'exist' in the same way that other beings or things (like people or chairs) 'exist'. But there are *all sorts* of ways of understanding the word 'God', such as God as the 'Ground-of-our-Being', or God as a sort of Ultimate Symbol or philosophical ideal, to be approached not in a woodenly literal way, but through imagination, using music, art and poetry.

There are many ways of believing in God, and if religion is to be a live option for far more people, Christians need to be a great deal bolder and more generous in their explorations and interpretations of the idea of God. Belief is a personal response to a set of data, and when faced with the same set of data one person may conclude one thing whilst another may conclude something completely different. To say, in effect, to someone that unless they are able to get their minds around some particular *version* of God they can't take religion seriously is arrogant, unimaginative exclusivism. If God is thought of, say, as a philosophical ideal, and if this acts as a ladder up which religious outsiders can climb, or a bridge across which they can pass, or a door through which they can go and find a religious home in the Church, that is truly wonderful and should be welcomed by more orthodox believers. After all, the idea or image of God that we use is only a tool, only a means to an end: if seen as anything else, it has become an idol (see Chapter 27).

It may come as a surprise to some to realise that such views of God are possible, if the only version of religion they know is the one heard in Sunday School. In all other areas of human thought we allow (and indeed *expect*) development: the understanding of physics of the primary school child is very different to that of the university student (see Chapter 37). But because adolescence usually marks the end of religious education (if in fact it ever got started) people get stuck in a sort of time warp. The good news is that there *is* religious life after Sunday School; the bad news is that we have to work at it!

Perhaps the best starting point for a sceptic is to think, not in terms of trying to 'believe in God' (to put it like that is to shut off all sorts of imaginative ways of imagining God) but to recognise that all of us have depths in ourselves, which is what is meant by the word 'soul' (see Chapter 14). These depths are what yearn for the profound and the glorious, and are not fed by the banal or the superficial. They are what is reached when we respond to music or art or poetry – or religion, which is a way of organising our search for what is most real or significant. Although many thoughtful and sensitive people are able to do without religion, they would be hugely impoverished if they tried to do without *any* sense of profundity in their lives.

Another way that the sceptic could be helped is by being invited to look at the various ways in which the word 'God' is used. Instead of focusing on the existence of an object, this requires her to get involved with the life of a faith community. If its activities (reflecting, singing, praying, reading, thinking, discussing) draw her into the community, then she can truly be said to have 'come to faith', without ever trying to 'believe that God exists' in some objective sense. Believing in God might be said to be 'falling in love with life'; afterwards, nothing seems the same again.

Churches need to become places where people gather, not to reinforce their certainties about a being called 'God', but to share in the experience of exploring ways of trying to satisfy their mutual spiritual hunger. The future for organised religion is bleak, unless we work at re-imagining and re-creating the idea of God (the God-*symbol*, if you like) so that it really *does* speak to the spiritual needs of our time.

Chapter 2

THINKING ABOUT THE BIBLE

There's some pretty odd stuff in the Bible! In fact, some of it is *so* odd that you wonder how it got in there in the first place. Part of the reason why it seems so strange is that it was written at a time when people thought very differently from the way we think today. Their understanding of the world was different, and their cultural practices were far removed from anything we would recognise. In acknowledging these differences, it has been well said that no one should ever simply read the Bible: you should either study it, or leave it alone.

The Bible is a collection of writings, mostly by unknown authors, with the earliest ones being written over a thousand years before the later ones. People often have a very black-and-white attitude to the Bible, and seem to think that the only choice is between accepting it all in a literal sense or rejecting it all. And given that some of the stories are clearly impossible (such as the wonderfully ludicrous one of Jonah living in the whale for three days), they dismiss the whole thing. But they don't have to. There's so much good stuff in the Bible that we need to reclaim the initiative from those whose approach to it is both unintelligent and unimaginative.

It's obviously not possible to be a Christian and *not* take the Bible seriously, but it *is* possible to be a Christian and not take the Bible *literally*. The problem is that lots of people are very touchy whenever questions are raised about the Bible, which makes it very difficult to get them to think (*really* think) about it at all! Whatever else it may be, the Bible is, first and foremost, a *religious book*: it's the story of the religious journey of a group of people over thousands of years; and it's also been (and remains) the core religious text of an enormous number of people over thousands of years. It's *about* religion – and it also *is* religion. Without it, the three great world monotheistic faiths wouldn't exist – which would leave a large hole in the spiritual lives of over half the world's people. It's therefore almost impossible to overestimate its importance.

The Bible is essentially a collection of old documents, written by a series of people – probably men – across many centuries. Few, if any, people would think of God as a sort of being who has a body and could therefore hold a pen and write things down. It would therefore be agreed that the Bible is a completely human book, in terms of its physical production. Many people, however, would want to say that although it was written by men, it was *inspired by God*, and is therefore the 'Word of God'. But what does this actually mean? How might God 'inspire' someone to write something? And how could we tell the difference between something that God has inspired someone to write, and something he hasn't? Has God inspired me to write this – or is it something that I've thought up all by myself? And if the latter, have I done so with (so to say) God's blessing, or with his disapproval? Simply raising the questions shows what tricky territory this is!

Is the claim that God (understood as a sort of super-person) dictated the words which unknown Bronze Age inhabitants of the Middle East then spoke (to whom and in what context?) and which eventually became passed down? Or is it that God somehow *thought* the words into the heads of people who then spoke or wrote them? Or what? The whole idea makes little sense to many people, but the Bible is so central to the development of Christianity (as well as Judaism and Islam) that we need in some way to mark it off as being special. Perhaps we can continue to call it the 'Word of God', so long as we make it clear that such a phrase is being used metaphorically rather than in a woodenly literal sense.

There's no getting away from the fact that the Bible is a very human book. It was not written by God, it was not edited by God, it was not translated by God. In the beginning, of course, it wasn't even written down at all. Most parts of the Bible started life as sayings or stories that were handed down from generation to generation as part of an oral tradition and doubtless became embellished in the process. Eventually they got written down, which tended to fix them a bit more, but before the invention of printing they were handed on by being copied out, and inevitably mistakes were made. And when they were translated from the original Hebrew, Aramaic and Greek, they suffered still further alteration because translation can never be exact.

Sir Alec Issigonis, the designer of the Mini, once famously commented that a camel is a horse designed by a committee, and the Bible is a bit like that! It's a book (in fact, a series of books) edited over the centuries by a committee, (in fact, a series of committees, from Hebrew scholars three hundred years before Jesus to leaders of the Christian Church in the fifth century) who decided which of the enormous numbers of religious writings in circulation were to be included. And just as the camel is a curious beast, so the Bible is a curious production. Some books (such as Revelation) might have been better left out, while other books might usefully have been included. It's all a matter of judgement – human judgement. *We're* the ones who decide which authorities to follow; and to say that a particular text is 'inspired by God' means that *we* happen to regard it as uniquely authoritative.

The miracle stories together with the Creation Story are a major problem to many people. This is because they strike at the very heart of our scientific understanding of the world. Miracles (see Chapter 12) seem to involve a suspension of the laws of nature, while the Creation Story seems to deny the Theory of Evolution. Of course scientists get things wrong (if they didn't, science could never progress) but there's something a bit desperate and sad about Fundamentalist Christians (see Chapter 28) trying to hang on to the literal view of the Creation Story in the face of all the evidence to the contrary.

Many thinking people find this anti-intellectualism the strongest possible reason to have nothing to do with Christianity – which is why those of us who are perfectly happy to go along with the scientific view of the world (what is the alternative?) need to make it clear that it is possible to take both the Bible *and* the modern world seriously. The bottom line is this: do you think that you can (and should) read the Bible literally – or not? If you do, you're saying that it is, in effect, the same sort of work as a physics textbook. If you don't think this then you're on a very slippery slope because once you allow that intelligence and critical faculties and awareness of metaphor have some part to play, there's no obvious point at which you can or should call a halt! You are then bound to ask questions like: which are the mythical bits? Which are the legendary bits? Which are the historical bits? Which are the metaphorical bits? And, what is most fundamental: *how can you possibly distinguish between them?*

In 1974 the singer Ralph McTell released a single, *The Streets of London*, a song about people you might encounter as you wandered around the capital. It was a pleasant enough, 'social-conscience' kind of song, and it was very popular. I came across it again a little while ago in a sketch on a comedy programme. The Ralph McTell character was singing the song in a nightclub, and when he finished the audience applauded warmly. He then introduced his next song – but the audience was aghast. They started shouting out: 'Streets of London! The Streets of London! ...' He said 'I've just sung it' – but they cried all the more 'Streets of London! The Streets of London! ...' Clearly baffled and upset he began his next song, but there was so much booing that eventually he stopped. To enormous relief and applause he then started to sing *The Streets of London* again – and presumably when he finished, he sang it again. And again.

This was both funny and sad. To be attached to something so much that you are not able to move on and try something new is life-denying – but it's what happens all too often in religion! Many people want (or perhaps it's more like 'crave' or 'need') to hear the same things said, in the same way, over and over again. The idea of exploring something new is anathema to them – indeed, some even consider it to be heresy, because surely everything that can be said has been said, and so the only reasonable thing to do is ... say it again!

The Church colludes in this, not least because such an approach allows it to control what goes on. But there's something monstrous and preposterous about it – as if Truth *could* be kept fettered in this way, a bit like thought was in Stalinist Russia. Religion is a profound human response to the Mystery of Life, and Christianity is one of its many forms. The Christian path is one that helps enormous numbers of people, but it demands a pretty dull and blinkered mind to assume that everything that can be said and thought on the subject has already been said and thought, and all that's left for us to do now is get on and believe it!

But, dull and blinkered though it is, this is the view that huge numbers of people seem to hold. And the problem is that they are what constitute the noisy core of Church religion – which means that anyone who sees things differently is bound to feel alienated from much that goes on in the Church. But just as Socialists may feel they ought to stay in the Labour Party (even though it's not much to their taste any more, it's better than the alternatives) so religious liberals (see Chapter 18) may feel that they need to stay in the Church (they need a spiritual home somewhere, and this seems the best one on offer).

The Bible is a magnificent book, with a huge list of characters, a strong central plot, and plenty of intrigue, betrayal, love and hate. Drama and poetry and bits of history are all mixed in, with some uplifting stuff and some very peculiar stuff as well. But provided we use our intelligence and don't try to read it all in the same way, the Bible contains enough inspiration and challenge to last anyone at least a lifetime.

Chapter 3

THINKING ABOUT THE CHURCH

Churches are, by definition, full of odd people – for the very good reason that going to church is an odd sort of thing to do. Years ago it was much more common, although nowhere near as common as is sometimes suggested – men in particular have always been conspicuous by their absence from church!

But why does *anyone* bother to go to church? It's a very real question, one that could be asked by tens of millions of people in this country – and perhaps would be if they ever bothered to think about it. Is there any sort of answer that will make sense to them? Indeed, is there any sort of answer that will make them more likely to think about going themselves? It all comes down to what the Church has to offer people. Why *should* someone go to church, rather than go to visit friends or relations, or watch a football match, or laze around and read the paper?

There are plenty of answers that **won't** do. The most obvious one is to say that *'we go to church to worship God – and because we ought to worship God, it follows that we (and indeed everyone else) ought to go to church'*. It's the sort of thing that religious people say, and because it's got two key religious words in it ('worship' and 'God') it sounds like the sort of thing they *ought* to say. But it's a hopeless answer, because it uses the kind of language that religious outsiders find so meaningless and such a turn-off. Part of the problem, of course, is that religion in

Britain, as in almost all of the rich countries, is such a minority interest, that those who take it seriously feel somewhat beleaguered, and tend to retreat into religious ghettoes (called churches) where they mix mainly with their own kind and speak to each other in their own special language. And although it is the very opposite of what Jesus did, when he got out and mixed with anyone and everyone, speaking to them in ways that made sense, it still seems to be almost irresistibly attractive to most of those who take religion seriously.

Of course, anyone who thinks about it would know that the answer 'to worship God' is inadequate. No one could seriously suggest that such an answer would be of the least use in helping a religious outsider to become a religious insider. Rather than being helpful such as answer is likely to sound like religious gobbledegook. But unless we talk to religious outsiders, or at least have a very good sense of imagination, we may easily fail to realise that their objections to going to church are a lot more deep-seated than simply a quibble about the form or the timing of the services. The only good reason for going to church is because you get something out of it: if you simply can't see any point in it you won't go.

To say this is to risk the ire of the traditionalists, whose view is that we don't go to church for our own benefit, but for God's benefit. But it is indisputable that unless someone gets *something* out of going to church they won't go again. That 'something' might be a sense of peace; it might be an opportunity for reflection; it might be a sense of mystery; it might be an awareness of the ways in which they need to change certain aspects of their own lives; it might be an enjoyment of the hymns and the organ; it might be a feeling of companionship; or whatever. All of these are worthy and valuable – *and what is significant is that none of them mentions the word 'God'!*

Church services are not entertainments (although some come perilously close!) and require *effort* from those attending. We need to be active and not passive, we need to work at trying to incorporate the ideas and challenges that are offered (or which come to us) during the services into our own lives. In the past, when church-going was much more common, it was considered by many to be the 'thing to do' on a Sunday. This may still occur in places, but most of the people who go now are there because it's important to them to be there.

At the very least the Church offers a way of celebrating and reinforcing the values that we hold in common. It offers an opportunity for exploring the really significant questions of life, by providing a framework created by earlier generations of Christians, which can serve as a starting point for our own contributions. And although the 'tradition of the Church' may contain, in addition to a lot of wisdom, a fair amount of prejudice and ignorance, it is a wonderful and priceless resource nevertheless. It's all too easy to get sucked into a spiral of busy-ness in our everyday lives, and sometimes we need a time of enforced stillness. Church services try to provide this, and encourage us to ask important questions which often get pushed to one side. What really matters to us? How do we see our lives? What are our priorities? Do they need revising?

All the great world religions focus on such questions, because they are the only ones that really matter. Unless we're careful we can get carried along by life, being passengers instead of trying to steer the craft. We can all too easily accept the role of couch potatoes, or even 'victims', instead of trying to make something really worthwhile of the time we've got. Increasing numbers of people go to therapists or counsellors or GPs to talk about matters which they might have been able to work through themselves had they been members of a church community. Church can't offer simple, instant solutions, but it can give us a framework within which we can begin to tackle the problems.

Most church services have a time to reflect on the ways in which we have fallen short of what we should have done and been. This doesn't mean that we have to feel wracked by guilt, but there's no point in trying to kid ourselves that we're beyond either criticism or hope. There will also be a time when passages are read aloud from the

Bible, and there will probably be a time when a sermon is given, usually related to one of the Bible passages. There will be a time of prayer when we focus on all sorts of matters of concern, and consider how we might best respond. And there may be hymns, some of which have odd words but good tunes! (or vice versa)

It's fortunate that there are so many brands of religion on offer, and even lots of brands of Christianity. This means that people can (and do) shop around, until they find the sort that appeals to them. Those who want what amounts to a self-contained religious world go somewhere different to those who need their religion to be completely integrated into the everyday. And just as vegetarians would gag on a steak, so some people would choke (or starve) on the sort of religious diet that seems to feed others.

People go to church for all sorts of reasons – and companionship is no less worthy a motive than theology! Although some may like the idea of going back in time when they go to church (and of course the age of many of the buildings, together with the language that is used and the vestments that are worn all help to suggest that religion operates in a sort of time warp) religion is essentially about looking forward, and church services should help us live our ordinary everyday lives more fully and lovingly and generously.

Those who simply can't see the point in reflecting on the big questions of life, or who find it tiresome or pointless to sit quietly for a while, or who have only a very short attention span, are unlikely to get much out of a church service. But those who think that life is too important to waste, and who feel that they need a time of stillness, may find that churches are able to provide a suitable forum to help them in their personal journeying, and to act as a much needed counterbalance to the self-centredness that is endemic in our society.

Chapter 4

THINKING ABOUT PRAYER

Those of us who spend a lot of time hanging around churches may easily forget just how odd religion must seem to anyone who never goes near one. Many of the people who turn up for baptisms, weddings or funerals look extremely uncomfortable, just as we would if we were in what seemed an alien environment. And perhaps the oddest thing of all in the service is when people close their eyes and pray. What are they actually doing?

It might seem to someone who just happened to wander into a church during the prayers that here was a group of people who had taken leave of their senses. And this shows just what an odd thing prayer actually is. It appears to be one side of a conversation (sometimes out loud, sometimes silently) with an invisible person, whose replies (if any) are inaudible. We've all come across people who wander along the street talking to no-one in particular, and find such a spectacle very sad. But this must be how *we* all look when we're praying!

Young children tend to join in with what grownups do, and may quite happily copy their parents if they are in the habit of praying. The children put their hands together, close their eyes, and say the appropriate words. But what's going on inside their heads when they do this? Do they think that they're talking to someone a bit like the

Invisible Man? Or perhaps it's someone like Father Christmas, who although obviously not invisible (we've seen enough pictures of him to know *that*!) is nevertheless so far away that communication has to be rather different from normal. Perhaps God is thought of as a Father Christmas figure with very acute hearing – so acute, in fact, that he can hear even when the prayers are only *thought* rather than said? It's all very mysterious – but then prayer *is* very mysterious. And it's also very troubling, in that lots of churchgoers feel like failures because they find prayer hard. Probably the main reason for this difficulty is that they wonder whether *anything* is actually happening when they pray. Or are they simply talking to themselves?

The way you understand prayer depends to a large extent on the way you understand God. If you are a 'theist' (someone who thinks of God as a separate being, existing in some sense independently of the world) then you will probably think of prayer as a sort of conversation. If you are a 'non-theist' (someone who thinks of God in a very different way – perhaps as the 'Ground of our Being', or as the 'sum of our values', or as the creative and healing power of love) then prayer will be more like an exploration into the mystery at the heart of human life. Sometimes a distinction is drawn between prayer and meditation, with the former being thought of as talking to someone else, whilst the latter is talking to oneself. But unless someone is a theist, there's no need to try and distinguish between them, and it's probably better not to. Many non-churchgoers may find the idea that prayer does **not** have to be thought of as an internal conversation with an external but invisible person to be puzzling, whilst many churchgoers may find the suggestion positively offensive. But there will be many others, both inside and outside the churches, who may find such an idea supremely liberating, because they can make no sense of the idea of such a being.

Prayer is traditionally divided up into four kinds: Adoration, Confession, Thanksgiving and Supplication. *Adoration* is our response to the awesome wonders of the world. *Confession* is confronting the uncomfortable reality that in all sorts of ways we fall short of what we ought to be. *Thanksgiving* is the expression of gratitude for the many blessings in our lives. *Supplication* (or Petition) is when we ask for things. If these are on behalf of others, it's known as *Intercession*, and this tends to be what comes to most people's minds when the subject of prayer is mentioned.

Someone we know may be desperately ill, and seems beyond medical help. The natural response of many people (even if religion normally plays no part whatsoever in their lives) is to pray that they will get better. It's a common response, and a campaign of prayer may be undertaken, with lots of people focusing on the needs of this particular sufferer – but there's something worrying about doing this if it's the theistic God that is being prayed to. It seems to be assumed that such a God has not only to be alerted to the needs of people, but also begged, coaxed and pleaded with if he is to do something about their problems. What sort of God would only make people better if and when enough other people asked hard enough? And what would it say about the (supposedly) infinite value of each and every person?

The idea of a God who has favourites is disgusting – but hardly surprising given that much of the language we use about God is exactly the same as that used of emperors and kings. It's the language of grovelling and cringing, and shows that we are still in thrall to the view of God as a fearful tyrant who needed to be placated by all sorts of 'offerings', in the form of animal (perhaps even human?) sacrifices that is found in much of the Old Testament. Today many people can no longer take such an idea seriously, just as many people can no longer take seriously the idea of a social hierarchy. Fewer and fewer are able to use, unselfconsciously, titles such as 'My Lord' or 'Your Worship' or 'Your Majesty' or 'Your Excellency', and this means that continuing to address God in this way helps to make religion in general (and prayer in particular) impossible for them.

It doesn't have to be like this! If I pray that God will cure someone who is very ill, and they then recover, I can perfectly reasonably say that my prayer has been answered – not in the sense that I think my prayer made any difference (they may have got better anyway), but in the sense that the outcome I wanted so desperately has come about. Prayer in this case is functioning as an *expression* of deep feeling, and its 'answering' occasions an expression of deep gratitude. To ask God for things is not like asking a person for things: it is to express our most profound longings.

There is no 'correct way' to pray. Part of the problem of prayer is that people feel the need to try to do something which works for others, but not for them. It has been well said that we should 'pray as we can, not as we can't', and in a congregation there may be as many ways of understanding prayer as there are people. Prayer clearly 'works', but not in the sense of bringing measurable results. We hear about those occasions when extraordinary cures have occurred after prayer has been offered, but not about the occasions (almost certainly far more) when such a thing did *not* happen. Prayer *works* in the sense of helping people to find some sort of inner peace.

The essence of prayer is relationship, and so to pray for another person is to be in a relationship with them. It is to care for them, to take them seriously. It is to oppose whatever diminishes them, which means working to overcome things such as poverty and prejudice. Prayer is the reaching out of one soul to another, the yearning of a soul to be at peace with the universe. Prayer is taking the gift of life seriously, and living as deeply, richly and fully as possible. Doing this means expressing our love and concern for others in thought, word and deed, and this has the power to bring wholeness to those around us. If I pray with a sick person and they recover, I will see that as an answer to my prayer, but this doesn't mean that I have to think a being called 'God' has 'done something'. I may say that the power of love, which was released or expressed in my presence and my prayer, is the cause of the person's recovery. God might not be an additional causal agent, but my prayer *has* been answered.

Although it's part of our Christian duty (and privilege) to pray, it's unlikely that even the most conservative Christian thinks that praying for these things, *and doing nothing more*, is of any value at all. Surely no-one would think that praying for them is an alternative to *working* for them? Prayer is simply the prelude to action; and so if I'm well-off, and surrounded by people who are starving, the solution to their problem is not for me to pray for them but to buy food for them!

Petitionary Prayer is offered in order to try and 'make a difference'. But it's not (as is often thought) an attempt to make a difference to God – that is, to try and get a being called 'God' to do something that he/she otherwise wouldn't have done. Rather, the difference is in ourselves, in that prayer is a way of helping us to reflect on our deepest desires and thus to order our priorities. If God really *is* active in us, then we can think of 'God answering prayer' to the extent that *we ourselves do something* about whatever it is that we are praying for. If God really *is* the creative power of love and joy and peace within us, then our prayer, our focusing on whatever concerns us deeply, may release from within *us* that power of love and joy and peace which makes a real difference to the world. Prayer is a way of keeping alive our sense of responsibility, our hunger for justice, our unwillingness to accept the status quo, our hope of making sense of life.

To be continually awe-struck by the world is to pray, in that it helps our souls to fly. To be aware of our failings is to pray, in that it helps our souls to grow. To be thankful is to pray, in that it helps our souls to shine. None of these kinds of prayer attempts to change the world, and none depend on the idea of an interventionist God. All of them reflect the fact that we have spiritual needs which only prayer can satisfy, and somehow we have to find a language in which this can be communicated to those outside the Church who for whatever reason think they cannot pray. Worship is prayer; just as any activity that engages the soul is prayer. To think of prayer solely (or even mainly) in terms of a shopping list is desperate, not least because it's so widespread. Prayer is nothing less than the foundation of the spiritual life, and we need therefore to 'pray without ceasing', as St Paul put it, with such reflection being as natural as breathing – and almost as important!

Chapter 5

THINKING ABOUT THE CREED

One creed or another is said at most Church of England services, and this unfortunately causes enormous problems to lots of people! There are three different creeds officially in use, but the one most people come across is the Nicene Creed. This began life as the deliberations of a group of theologians and politicians at the Council of Nicaea in 325, who were called together to come up with a party line as to what Christians believed. After they all went home, the debate continued, and the creed didn't arrive in its final form until the Council of Constantinople in 381.

Like all the creeds it forms a convenient shorthand summary of traditional Christian belief, and is therefore useful as a way of reminding ourselves of what we're officially about. But as an introduction to Christianity, or as a help to faith, it's pretty useless, for two reasons:

(i) It *puts in* all sorts of claims that most people (including many churchgoers) couldn't even *begin* to accept as true in any historical or factual sense. This is why lots of those who attend church either keep quiet during the time when it's said, or have a pause when it gets to a bit they find particularly unhelpful (or even offensive), or say it but have a bad conscience about being hypocritical!

(ii) It *leaves out* almost everything that's really important. There is *nothing* in it that we can relate directly to our everyday living, nothing about the need to love and care for one another. In fact it is a summary, not of Christianity, but of *Churchianity*; an introduction to what counts as orthodoxy ('right thinking') rather than orthopraxis ('right living'). It contributes mightily to the idea that Christianity is a matter of the head rather than the hands, and that the way to salvation is through doctrine.

So what can we do about it? The easiest thing, of course, would be for the Church to stop saying it altogether. It doesn't have to – *we* don't have to. The only necessity in religion is what people put there. Creeds were invented *by* people, *for* people and can be scrapped (or ignored) by other people if they/we want to! Their use in our liturgy is a matter of choice – *our* choice. There's nothing God-given either about their words or the use to which those words are put. Indeed we might well ask, *do we actually need creeds at all?*

Any creed is as much a product of its time as a piece of old pottery, and it's important to remember that when we say one, we don't have to try and pretend that we see things in the same way as the people who wrote it. Some people (perhaps *many* people?) manage this without undue difficulty, but probably rather more find it impossible, and indeed, undesirable. The world has moved on a long way in the last 1700 years, and our understanding of almost everything has changed out of all recognition.

It might be that if the creeds were set to music they would cause fewer problems! After all, we sing lots of hymns with the most peculiar ideas, but if they have good tunes then the words may not matter much. The problem of the creeds is the problem of many other areas of Christianity: the clammy hand of the faith of the past can all too easily reach up and threaten to squeeze the life out of the faith of the present. If we are serious in our wish to see the continuation of Christianity, we must do whatever we can to try and ensure that this doesn't happen.

Many of the ideas in the creeds have done sterling work over the centuries, even the millennia, but they may now have become prisons in which contemporary expressions of spirituality are locked away. It has been well said that 'the past has a vote, not a veto', and we need to try to put ourselves into the shoes of those for whom conventional religious language has gone dead (or indeed has *always been* dead). The Buddha told a parable about a raft: a traveller comes to a wide stretch of water; the side he is on is dangerous, but the other side is safe. However, there is no bridge or boat. So he collects grass, sticks and branches to make a raft, and crosses to the other side. Because the raft has been so useful, he lifts it on to his head and carries it with him forever. The Buddha tells his followers that the traveller should have left the raft behind. It has served its purpose, and can now only be a hindrance. In this spirit, they should let go, not only of false teachings, but also of good ones.

This is almost unheard of in the Church! Doctrines and creeds grow by process of accretion: more keep getting added, and no one is brave enough to jettison the ones that are no longer helpful. But why not? To cling so tightly to the past is to show, not great faith, but a *lack* of faith. As an historical religion Christianity is always going to have a problem with old understandings of the faith. Like our religion, we are *products* of our past – but we don't have to be *prisoners* of it as well. The understanding of the faith preserved (fossilised?) in the creeds is historically important, but can never be the last word. In religion, *nothing* can ever be the last word: to quote T S Eliot, 'we must be still and still moving, into **another** intensity'.

Leslie Houlden refers to the Nicene Creed as the 'rugger song of the church', and this is a wonderfully irreverent and perceptive remark. It reminds us that when we say it we are, in effect, stating 'I'm a member of that gang', and proclaiming our solidarity with this particular group; we're subscribing to its general outlook, just as we do when we sing the National Anthem. In other words, when we say it we're not (or at least we don't have to *think* that we are) stating a series of religious propositions, but rather endorsing the fact that we are part of a community of fellow enquirers linked through the creed across space and time. Archbishop William Temple said that when he recited the creed he mentally prefaced it with the words 'I am prepared to live my life *as if* ...' There's a lot of this *'as if'* business in Open Christianity, for the very good reason that it means the priceless spiritual resources of the past are available to us on terms that do not undermine our intellectual integrity.

The danger of creeds is that they tempt people into thinking that the story is over, and all we're required (indeed all that we're *allowed*) to do is keep replaying it, over and over again. In fact, the story is new for each generation who have the task of continuing and re-presenting the faith in terms that resonate with their own time. The number of 'timeless truths' of religion is very small – and they're usually wrapped up in historical packaging that masks what's underneath.

Anyone who demands that 21st century Christians take literally the words of the creeds is consigning Christianity to the dustbin of history. Those who are unwilling to see this happen have a duty to make it known as widely as possible that things don't have to be like this; that it *is* possible to be a thinking Christian, and use religious symbols imaginatively and creatively. The creeds are pointers to the faith of the past: it's up to us to be pointers to the faith of the future.

Chapter 6

THINKING ABOUT HOLY COMMUNION

Most members of most Church of England congregations are middle-aged or older, and this isn't surprising given that the 1960s marked a cultural and religious watershed. Those growing up then were much less likely than earlier generations to have any interest in organised religion, a trend that has become more and more marked ever since. And although there are no grounds for supposing that it will ever be reversed, there *are* reasons for thinking that a lot more people might find Christianity worth bothering with if it were possible to understand it in a variety of ways. At present, as congregations shrink, there is a tendency for a fortress-mentality to take hold, with fewer and fewer people believing things more and more fervently. This serves only to reinforce the downward spiral. What is needed is a genuine enthusiasm for a variety of voices, so that insights from across the spectrum can be heard and shared.

If the Church is serious about wanting to share its riches with others, it needs to look at the implications of the fact that the number of church outsiders is increasing fast. Fewer and fewer of these have any real idea what goes on inside the building, and given that Holy Communion is the main Sunday service in most Anglican churches particular attention needs to be paid to making this as accessible and comprehensible as possible (without at the same time destroying its nature). It needs to be recognised that the Communion service may act as a very effective agent of *anti*-evangelism, because although the liturgy has great power and beauty, unless there is a basic sympathy with and understanding of what is going on, the outsider may conclude that the whole thing is unacceptably weird.

This means that Holy Communion will become a possible option for many outsiders, *only* if the Church is prepared to look openly and honestly at some of the questions that may be asked about it. Each of the different names for the service brings out a slightly different aspect: 'Holy Communion' comes from the communal sharing of bread and wine; 'the Lord's Supper' comes from the origin of the service (the Last Supper); 'the Mass' comes from the final words of the old Latin service, which 'sent' people out into the world; 'the Eucharist' comes from the Greek word for 'thanksgiving'.

The Last Supper wasn't just any old meal, of course: it was the 'Passover meal' that Jesus was eating with his disciples. This derives from the account in Exodus of how the angel of death, on its tour of Egypt to kill all the first-born, would 'pass over' those houses which had lamb's blood smeared on the doorposts. Each household then ate the lamb, and made good their escape from the Egyptians. The Passover story is in itself pretty odd, and introduces some rather troubling notions of God, including the idea that he had favourites. But things got a whole lot odder when the symbolism of this meal was *itself symbolised* in terms of the death of Jesus, who was seen as the Paschal lamb, the innocent victim who needed to die if others might escape.

The idea of 'sacrifice' is a problem for many; it made sense to Jews of 2000 years ago, but not to us today. The entire Communion service is soaked in the language of sacrifice, with the bread being (or 'standing for') Christ's body, and the wine his blood. The bread is broken just as his body was broken on the cross; it is then given just as his broken body was 'given for us', whilst the wine shows how his life-giving blood was 'poured out for us'. Many people find the service so powerful that they attend Communion every day, but others find the whole thing primitive and disgusting, and cannot get over its apparently cannibalistic aspects. As with any ritual the only real way to understand it is to take part in it, and to do so often enough that it becomes part of oneself: but for some this is impossible.

Cannibalism is based on the idea that through eating another human being it is possible to acquire his strength and courage. It is therefore a ritualistic act, and not simply a case of eating whatever food happens to be close to hand. Jews found the idea of drinking blood completely abhorrent, and therefore the idea that Jesus really *did* commend this practice to his disciples poses all sorts of problems. Old Testament references to people being eaten refer to the threats posed by enemies, and the way that by devouring someone it is possible to destroy them utterly. It might be that Jesus offered bread and wine to his disciples, in a perfectly normal way, and when they had eaten and drunk said to them 'you've just eaten and drunk *me*. It's people like *you* who are responsible for what's about to happen to me; it's people like *you* I'm going to die for'. Such an idea is unlikely, but so are all the other possible interpretations.

Apart from the Roman Catholic doctrine of transubstantiation (which says that in the Eucharist the bread and wine actually become, **literally**, the body and blood of Christ) any understanding of the Eucharist is necessarily symbolic – and none the worse for that. Symbolism is the way we deal with the most profound aspects of human life, which is why it's odd that many people are so reluctant to see religion as a profound system of symbols, and keep trying to literalise it. But in the case of the Eucharist, even if it's accepted that the whole thing *is* a matter of symbolism, the underlying cannibalistic ideas are still there – and does saying that we've *symbolised the cannibalism* make it acceptable? To the outsider, as well as to many of the insiders, the whole thing is bizarre. Smearing blood on doorposts sounds like magic, whilst eating the flesh of God may sound ludicrous and blasphemous, as well as cannibalistic. The further idea that unless ordained people preside over the service, the whole thing is inefficacious – it doesn't 'work' – is the final straw for many.

It may be that the Eucharist can be made much more accessible *only* if the Church starts to take symbolism seriously. Perhaps only in this way can it move beyond the idea that it is involved with magic, and that a special person saying certain special words can achieve some extraordinary result. It doesn't really matter *how* the Eucharist came into being; neither does it really matter *what* meaning it had in the past. The only important consideration is *whether* the Eucharist is able to have a meaning for a lot more people today than is currently the case. If not, the Church will continue its decline – perhaps rightly so.

Taking symbolism seriously will mean that in addition to all those who currently find the Eucharist a unique source of spiritual nourishment, someone who can make no sense of the God of theism will be able to participate fully in it. A performance of a play or an opera is not in the slightest devalued by the lack of historicity of the subjects. What matters is that a sense of atmosphere is created which allows the audience to immerse themselves in it. The Eucharist can be understood as a great drama, with people being invited, not to watch, but to be part of it. It isn't possible to understand the power of the Eucharist vicariously. The sharing of a common cup (in those places that still do this) is often thought of as unhygienic as it can lead to all sorts of germs being passed around. This in itself helps to reinforce the sense of occasion, because it's the sort of thing that most people wouldn't dream of doing normally. We need to be brought up short and reminded that sharing can be costly.

The language of the Eucharist is essentially that of sacrifice, and although this is not the sort of language that people use any more, nothing less than extreme language is capable of doing the job. If we really *are* serious about the need to change ourselves and the world, nothing less than everything can ever be enough. To 'give oneself' in the service of others requires the strongest, most extreme language that we can find. If we actually *do* go out into the world determined to *be* the Body of Christ, determined to try and love others, determined to make a difference, the Eucharist will have done its transforming work.

As the most obviously ritualistic service in the Church, the Eucharist is the occasion where a sense of the 'numinous' (the 'Other') is most likely to be found. But this can only happen if attention is paid to creating the right atmosphere. Times of silence are crucial, which is why an all-singing, all-dancing, entertainment-type Eucharist, the sort that would keep children and those of limited attention spans happy, is inappropriate. When someone comes into church for the service they should find an air of expectancy: a sense that something very special is about to happen. The liturgy should lead to a gradually increasing sense of tension, which reaches a high point in the Eucharistic prayer, when bread is offered, broken and given. By the time people come to receive/make their communion, the atmosphere should be positively electric.

We live in a society of rapid travel, fast food and instant entertainment. There will always be those who eat junk food, watch mindless television, and read tabloid newspapers; if they have any inclination towards religion it's only natural that they might expect it to be available in the same sort of way. Their needs are already well catered for, but there will also always be those (a much smaller number to be sure) who are more discerning and want good food, high culture – and thoughtful, demanding religion. As the very heart of our worship, the Eucharist is where they should be fed: it is the task of the Church to ensure that they receive living bread and not simply pap.

Chapter 7

THINKING ABOUT BAPTISM

Most people go nowhere near a church, except for special occasions such as baptisms. A century ago almost three quarters of babies were brought for baptism; now it is less than one quarter. But even this much-reduced figure means that many of those for whom religion seems to play no part in their everyday lives still want their babies baptised. It might be that they have some dormant religious sense, or it might be that baptism is seen simply in social terms as a rite of passage, being a sort of 'naming ceremony' and an opportunity for a family party to mark the birth.

The arrival of a new baby *is* a wonderful event that needs to be gloriously celebrated, and the ritual of baptism provides the occasion for doing this. The preciousness and fragility of life is especially evident in the case of babies, and the awesome responsibility of trying to guide and nurture them makes most parents feel grossly inadequate. Religion is a response to the terror and the mystery and the grandeur of the universe in which we find ourselves, and provides a language and a setting in which we can express our deepest fears and longings, especially those surrounding matters of life and death.

There may be something almost sacramental about the family party that usually follows the baptism. Gathering together to share and to celebrate is what happens at the Eucharist, and is a key way of building and strengthening the bonds of the church community. Ordinary families need to be cherished in the same sort of way, and the party is therefore an important occasion in its own right.

But baptism *is* a lot more than an opportunity for a party. There is almost bound to be a sense in which the parents, in effect, want 'something of God' to touch their baby. Birth is such an amazing event it is hardly surprising if many people find that only religion can provide a way of responding that is anything like adequate. People outside the Church may be completely unaware of the theology surrounding baptism, with all its associations of water washing away the stain of sin, but this is hardly the point. When parents ask for baptism they want the Church to welcome and value their baby, and it is vital that it does this in a positive way. Although there is a separate service of 'Thanksgiving for the Gift of a Child', most people see this as second rate – and therefore, by definition, not what they want, which is that their baby receives the very best of everything. But although these are highly laudable sentiments, they have the potential to lead to all sorts of problems!

Strictly speaking, baptism is the admission of a person to membership of the Christian Church, but *in practice* it tends (for most families) to be essentially a Thanksgiving service, with the Christian initiation aspect of much less significance. The gap between theory and practice upsets the liturgical and ecclesiological purists, because they say that for the Church to collude in what is a very significant change of meaning represents a caving-in to the forces of secularism. It's the usual unprincipled and infinitely flexible liberal suspects who are responsible for this of course, but all they're doing is carrying on what has been the practice of the Church of England for many centuries. It used to be that parents were *required* to bring their babies for baptism as soon as possible after birth, without any real concern about the nature of either their intentions or beliefs, and therefore without any investigation as to the likelihood of the baptismal promises being carried out. This 'open baptism' policy has penetrated into the culture very deeply, and any attempt to make it more restrictive or conditional is bound to have severe repercussions in terms of people's attitude to the Church.

The fact that baptism can be seen in these two different ways shows how the postmodern linguistic flux (see Chapter 21) has set us both free and adrift, and resulted in ambiguity all round. If word meanings (such as 'baptism') are not to be seen as static, then there is bound to be confusion when the way they are used changes. Inevitably the old and new meanings end up running in tandem, with disputes about which one is 'correct'. The temptation to ask such a question is strong, but needs to be resisted, because it implies a fixity of meaning, which has never been the case. And despite the inevitable fulminations of those who find such a flux disturbing, this is the nature of the world we live in, and we need to come to terms with it.

Christianity may be taken seriously without taking it literally, and the religious liberal (see Chapter 18) would obviously be hugely sympathetic to any parent or godparent who said that they could only make sense of the baptismal promises if they were understood in a metaphorical sense. It would be both presumptuous and uncharitable to assume that all non-churchgoers are unable to make the promises with integrity, and liberals will want to look for ways in which the parents and godparents can be helped towards an understanding of baptism that starts from where they are, and tries to find ways in which it can be made to resonate with the people who intend to make the promises. But while this is important, the underlying challenge of Christianity must not be lost in the process. The parents and godparents should feel that the Church is interested in them and is more than happy to celebrate the birth of their baby; but unless they *also* take away with them some idea of what Christianity is all about, an opportunity will have been lost.

The promises require the parents and godparents to do more than try to be nice people (which is hard enough); they also say that they will try to be *Christian* people (which is even harder). Attempting to live according to Christian principles means focusing on self-giving love, an example of which would be to put our responsibilities before our rights. It's not possible to take Christianity seriously unless it really *does make a difference* to the way life is lived, which is why it needs to be made clear to the parents and godparents that there should be real and identifiable changes in how they live.

It is very muchto be hoped that those who make the promises will come to church regularly, and will encourage the child for whom they have responsibility to do the same. Some churches require that parents attend church over a period of months before consideration can be given to baptising the baby, but the most likely result of such a policy is a sharp decline in the number of requests that are made for baptism. The ideal of regular attendance should be presented, together with specific invitations to services that the members of that particular family are likely to find most accessible. Whether or not they subsequently come (and most will probably appear at the crib and Christingle services) baptism provides a point of contact with families which otherwise wouldn't exist, and is the beginning of a relationship that needs to be nurtured.

What goes on inside the heads of the parents and godparents (i.e. their beliefs) is a lot less important than the fact that baptism helps them to take the first tentative steps towards being part (albeit in a loose sense) of a Christian community, and to begin to explore (albeit ever so gently) the faith that that community tries to live by. In an ideal world, of course, the parents and godparents would already be fully paid-up church attenders, but that's not the world we actually live in. We *must* make the most of the opportunities presented by the 'occasional offices' to keep the rumour of God alive in our society.

Chapter 8

THINKING ABOUT MARRIAGE

Religious Fundamentalists, together with those who have sternly fixed moral principles, must find the way that so many young couples live together ('in sin') before getting married (or perhaps even *without* getting married) very distressing. In the past such goings-on were very much the exception – and probably a source of family scandal. Nevertheless even today most couples eventually *do* marry, despite all the expense involved. Why do they bother? And given that most of them live without any reference at all to religion, why do so many of them choose to get married in church? Is the church simply an attractive backdrop for the photos, or is there something more going on?

Weddings in general, and church weddings in particular, involve an enormous fuss. Plans are made months, sometimes years, in advance, and amount to a major logistical operation usually costing thousands of pounds. Details of the wedding dress, the bridesmaids, the photographer, the reception, the honeymoon and so on need to be carefully planned. And in amongst all this, the bit in the church needs some thought as well! Churches are special places, with an atmosphere all their own, and this is universally accepted irrespective of whether people are religious or not. It is atmosphere that makes the difference between something ordinary and something very special, and this is so with respect to all sorts of places – Glen Coe has it,

Stonehenge has it, even the old Wembley Stadium had it. Places acquire atmosphere as a result of their association with momentous events. And having acquired it, so long as those events are preserved in our collective memory, they will keep it. Churches are holy places, set aside for especially significant occasions. The great human dramas take place here: the baptism service celebrates the beginning of new life; the marriage service marks a new relationship in the community; the funeral service is the occasion for giving thanks at the end of life. Because human life is sacred, the fact that churches are places where the extremes of human experience are recognised and expressed means that the building acquires a sacredness or 'specialness' of its own.

There's no reason to suppose that there's anything 'objective' about this: it's unlikely ever to register on a piece of scientific equipment. But that's neither here nor there: the important point is that such things matter to human beings, who as far as we know are the only meaning-making creatures around. It's obvious that the most important day of two people's lives needs to be celebrated in the most special way possible, and this means being in the most special *place* possible: the most *meaning-filled* place possible. And although increasing numbers of people are getting married in such places as country houses, a church wedding is what very large numbers of people still want, even if they normally have no interest in churchy things.

Lots of people don't have much of an idea what Christianity is about, and given that a church wedding may be their first brush with it, it's good that such an occasion is about the best possible introduction to it. This is because the two things at the heart of marriage are the same two things at the heart of Christianity: *love and commitment*. People sometimes seem to think that religion is a sort of odd hobby, something for the seriously sad and weird to do on a Sunday. In fact it's a way of helping us to focus ourselves, our whole lives, on Love – the same reason why we go to weddings, which are a public statement and celebration that Love is the most important thing that there is. And this is why it's worth making the most enormous fuss we can.

At the heart of any marriage is Love: without it, there obviously wouldn't be a wedding in the first place. And the central theme of the Christian faith is that Love is the Ultimate Reality, that Love conquers everything, that Love is all that matters. Therefore in the giving and receiving of Love we get a glimpse of what Ultimate Reality is like, of what really matters – in other words, we get a glimpse of God. God is Love; where Love is, God is. These aren't slogans, but the very core of Christianity. They show that our ordinary lives can be transformed into something quite extraordinarily beautiful as a result of the giving and receiving of Love. But of course we can only love other people by opening ourselves to them, and doing this makes us vulnerable. It's a risky, scary thing to do, but without it no meaningful relationship is possible.

Love is obviously crucial, but marriage isn't just about love: it's also about commitment. It's two people who cannot bear to be apart agreeing to join their lives together, with all that that entails. Not simply whilst it's pleasant or convenient, or until something better comes along, but forever. It's this level and depth of commitment, announced in a very public way in church, which demonstrates the sincerity of the two people concerned. If they are simply living together, the arrangement can be terminated relatively easily, although doubtless accompanied by a mixture of pain and acrimony. Making vows in church is an example of what are sometimes called 'performative utterances', when simply saying (performing) the words makes something happen. The bride and the groom make their promises to one another, and it is this action, in that context, which constitutes their marriage. The vicar *announces* that they are 'man and wife', but by the time those words are said, they are married. Context is all-important, requiring both a legally recognised place and officiant: the words alone aren't sufficient.

All church services depend on context: the combination of place and officiant make it clear that something significant is going on. The things that are said in the course of such services resemble performative utterances more than they resemble factual reports. To confess one's sins or to praise God or to pray for the sick or to say the creed are all meaning-filled, meaning-full activities; the simple fact of saying them reverently and seriously means that they succeed in what they are trying to do. If an unbeliever dismissed such things as ridiculous, and akin to writing notes to Father Christmas, it would show a complete lack of understanding of the sorts of activities they were. Unlike the requests for presents, what we say in church can be said without any anticipation of reward: we praise God because we are brimming over with joy, and so on. In the same way that pain-language *expresses* (not reports) our pain (which can be very real, perhaps almost unbearable) God-language *expresses* our joy or our sorrow or our terror or our sense of awe (which can all be very real, perhaps almost unbearable). In the marriage service the couple commit themselves to behaving in a particular way, which is at the core of *every* church service: a resolution to live in a particular way, according to certain principles.

The Church has traditionally taken a rather dim view of the institution of marriage, with it being seen as very much a second-best. Celibacy was the preferred option, but marriage was available for those who couldn't manage it. St Paul commented that 'it is better to marry than to burn' and this was echoed in the words of the Prayer Book service, which noted that marriage 'was ordained for a remedy against sin, and to avoid fornication ... (for those) as have not the gift of continency'. In other words, marriage is better than fornication (any form of sexual activity outside marriage) – but only just! It wasn't something to be entered into joyfully and lustily, but soberly and even shamefully, because wanting to be married was an admission that a person lacked the self-control (of both body and mind) that genuine celibacy required. Such a view seems bizarre today, but the negative attitude of Christianity to sex (see Chapter 22) lingers on in all sorts of ways.

Marriage and Christianity *both* require us to take our responsibilities to others with the utmost seriousness; there are no shortcuts, and there are bound to be many times when we fail. In an age when people talk a great deal about their rights, and very little about their responsibilities, the ideas and ideals of unconditional love and commitment and responsibility are deeply unfashionable. But each of them provides a wonderful opportunity to help people grow into more beautiful human beings and, as such, each of them is a route to God.

Everyone in England has the right to be married in their parish church, with no questions asked about what they happen to believe. The vicar may well make enquiries about this, but the answer given will in no way affect the ability of the couple to marry. And despite the protests of some this is surely as it should be. Religious belief is *not* what is important at a wedding: what really matters is a genuine commitment to one another. If this is present, it will in itself make the occasion a serious, love-filled, meaning-filled affair: and where Love is, God is.

Chapter 9

THINKING ABOUT FUNERALS

'Sometimes I sit in church and think "this is complete bollocks, all of it, and always has been," and then a month later I'd sit there thinking "this is all there is"'.

(Ian Hislop)

As the editor of *Private Eye*, Ian Hislop makes a living out of saying things that many people don't really want to hear, and his observations about the Church are likely to cause outrage, not least because for many there may be the sneaking sense that he's spot on. If there *is* any truth in what he says, it's probably at funerals when the greatest number of people are likely to describe the proceedings as 'complete bollocks'. This is partly because everyone goes to funerals, and therefore funeral congregations, as a cross section of the population, include large numbers of non-churchgoers; and partly because the things that are said at funerals are so very extraordinary.

Some 600,00 people die in Britain each year, three quarters of them in hospitals, hospices or residential homes. At least half of all those who die either have no belief whatsoever in life after death, or at best are very uncertain about it. Similar views are bound to be held by members of funeral congregations, which means that the language and ideas used at most funeral services (how we can look forward with confidence to eternal life; how we know that our dear departed brother/sister is in the hands of God, etc.) sound like a lot of baloney to at least half of those present, and often probably a lot more. This is an uncomfortable reality that the Church has to take on board if it wants to engage with where people actually are, rather than where many of the clergy would *like* them to be. Continuing to talk 'complete bollocks', especially on such sensitive occasions, is not an option if the Church wants to be taken seriously.

Most funerals are taken by members of the clergy, even if the deceased had rarely, if ever, set foot inside a church. Given the lack of religious belief on the part of most people, it's perhaps surprising that clergy aren't asked more frequently to conduct non-religious funeral services: some will agree and some won't, but many people might not even know that such things are a possibility. In an important sense, of course, the funeral isn't for the person who has died, but for his/her family and friends, and so the key question is not whether the deceased was religious, but whether the service is helpful to those who have come to 'pay their respects'. The body language of many members of funeral congregations suggests that they are both unfamiliar and uncomfortable with much that goes on in the service, and this is hardly surprising if it all sounds to them like gobbledegook.

Funerals are occasions when the worlds of church and secular society meet particularly sharply. At ease in both crematorium and church, the clergy can be seen smiling and casually greeting the familiar figures of organist and other staff. The mourners by comparison are at a double disadvantage, in that they are carrying a burden of grief, and they are in an alien environment. The job of the clergy is to ensure the service is conducted with dignity, and to say things that will be of value to those who are present. In particular it is their job to try and bring life out of death, to try and help the mourners come to terms with what has happened, and then to be in a position to start to move on.

A funeral is bound to be a time of mixed feelings, not least because people are trying to look backwards as well as forwards. They look backwards as they remember, and although the memories are bound to be a mixture of happy and sad, the overall sense of loss may be almost overwhelming. But they are also encouraged to look forwards: having valued the past, they need to reach out to the future and re-enter the stream of life, although this is obviously a lot easier said than done. A funeral is an opportunity to celebrate, to reminisce, to laugh and to cry together. It is way of recognising the fact that a particular human being has passed this way, and will not do so again. It is entirely right that death should be marked in a solemn way, because it is about the most solemn thing that there is. The life of a human being has ended, and the momentousness of the occasion needs appropriate expression.

The value of a set liturgy is that it brings dignity and order into a situation where everything else may seem to be falling apart. Sometimes one or two friends or family will stand up at the funeral and 'say a few words', but all too often the whole process is rushed through at the specific request of the family. Clergy are frequently asked not to say too much because 'Fred didn't want a fuss to be made'. This may be true: but it may also be true that those attending the service can't easily face the prospect of being in too close a proximity to the reality of death for very long. Many take little or no part in the service, neither singing the hymns nor saying 'Amen' at the end of the prayers. And although being a spectator at a funeral is perhaps a way of distancing oneself from the awesomeness of death, it isn't going to help people come to terms with their loss, or indeed with their own mortality, which at funerals stares everyone in the face.

It comes back to the question of alienation. Very few people have much in the way of what might be thought of as 'conventional' (which it isn't anymore) religious belief, and so a service whose address and prayers emphasise judgement and everlasting life, heaven and hell, is bound to fail to connect with all of the many people there who can make no sense at all of such ideas. Given that such large numbers find the language and concepts of the service less than helpful, the Church needs to explore ways of finding/giving meaning to the words used that actually resonate with those present, as well as looking to see whether new words and ideas would do the job even better.

People are bound to wonder if they will ever see Fred again, and the only honest answer is that no one knows. Some people are convinced as to the reality (and nature) of life after death; others are convinced that the idea is total nonsense, and a triumph of wishful thinking. Each group holds their view sincerely and with great conviction, but they obviously can't both be right. This ambiguous situation needs to be recognised, rather than, as is so often the case, pretending that it doesn't exist, or assuming that those whose views run counter to the Church's traditional teaching are simply wrong.

The current situation demands that if members of funeral congregations are to participate fully in the service they must, in effect, be able to pass a doctrinal test: those who cannot subscribe to the requisite number of beliefs, are effectively disenfranchised from the religious element. This is, of course, the really important part: not in the dogmatic sense, but in the sense that unless the service honestly reflects their hopes and fears, their doubts and unbeliefs, unless it has in short *some* sort of spiritual framework that rings true for them, they are not being provided with a context within which they can set the life and death of their loved one. And in turn this means that they may *not* leave the service able and willing to assert life over death.

This sense of alienation from the funeral rites is reflected (and probably exacerbated) by the fact that about three quarters of funerals take place not churches but in the local crematorium. And however hard these may try, they never manage to look or feel like churches. Their very location counts against them: churches are often at the heart of their communities, whilst crematoria are either on the edge of town or even in the middle of the countryside. They stand apart, isolated from the people they exist to serve. Lacking any sense of the mysterious or the sacred, they operate a remorseless, production-line system which simply adds to the general failure to do justice to this most momentous of occasions. In the majority of churches the coffin stands at the foot of the chancel steps, the place where couples are married and where parents and godparents make baptismal promises; a funeral is but one of many significant services that take place there, each one marking some major human occasion. The contrast with crematoria, whose sole business is death, could not be greater, and simply reinforces the sense that dying is not really part of the human condition, but a peculiar aberration.

Unless the Church finds a way of speaking about death and resurrection in terms that make some sort of sense to most of the people who attend funeral services, it will continue to be seen as a bizarre irrelevance. But it will only manage this if it tries a lot harder to get alongside the bereaved in their belief (or lack of belief) as well as recognising and respecting the views of the deceased. Simply to bang the orthodox drum as loudly as possible on such occasions, in the hope that the noise will drown out everyone's discomforting doubts, is hopeless. And because the current approach sits so ill with where most people actually are, it means that the Church continually fails to provide the help that it should be doing as the bereaved begin to come to terms with what is a new, and potentially very empty version of normal life.

Chapter 10

THINKING ABOUT CHRISTMAS

There's a lot of cynicism around at Christmas, but that's hardly surprising because there's a lot of it around the rest of the year as well. People complain about the commercialism, about the vulgarity, about the crowds, about the prices. However, given that it tends to be the same people who complain about all of these things (and more) it suggests that the problem is with them rather than with Christmas itself.

Christmas is a marvellous mixture of the profound and the tacky, the sacred and the secular, the hedonistic and the generous. In other words it's a bit like each of us, who have so many different facets that we're about as hard to sum up as Christmas. It's a time of wonder and yearning, and although it coincides with the pagan mid-winter festival, its symbolism is enormously richer. There aren't many people so hard-bitten that they aren't moved by the birth of a baby, a bearer of new hopes, new dreams and new beginnings. The historical baby Jesus was born a very long time ago; and like all births it was a once-and-for-all thing, never to be repeated. The Jesus of faith, however, is free of such constraints. Through the medium of our imagination he can, and is, born again each and every year, as the focus of *our* new hopes, new dreams and new beginnings.

Christmas touches us profoundly because it takes us back to our childhood, when the world was new and exciting, a time when we

61

hadn't learned to be sophisticated and cynical. We love Christmas carols because we learned them when we were young, at a time when Christmas was special beyond words. Whenever we hear them, therefore, we are reminded, at a very deep level, of a precious and safe time that is charged with all sorts of wonderful associations.

But we can only fully appreciate the Christmas stories if we look at them through the eyes of faith, and take them at face value. It's not a question of pretending to believe something we don't really believe, any more than immersing ourselves in a Shakespearian tragedy means trying to convince ourselves that it is all historically true. But it *does* mean trying to recapture the sense of wonder that we felt as children, when our imagination was firing on all cylinders, and the world was full of infinite possibilities. Religion and imagination are always intertwined, and their combination gives us the ability us to transcend ourselves, and discover (or, more properly, *re*-discover) the wonder that we once had but which is in danger of being smothered by the world-weariness that is all around (and inside) us.

Churches are a lot fuller at Christmas than they usually are, which shows that great numbers of people feel that the season wouldn't be complete without some sort of religious input. The problem is that when they come to one of the services they are likely to be told that the central message of Christmas is that it's a celebration of the coming of God to earth – *but for the life of them, they can't make any sense of such a claim*. And so they probably go away thinking that although they can *just* about manage a dose of religion once a year, the rest of the time it's best left to those who like that sort of thing – you know, people who can cope with odd ideas.

If this *is* how some people think, it's a great pity, because it's based on a huge mistake. Christianity *isn't* simply a collection of odd ideas, unless you count taking other people's needs seriously as an odd idea. The teaching of the Church is that it's in the story of Jesus (not the story of his birth, but the story of the way that he lived and died) that we see what is most worthy, what is most true, what is of ultimate value – and it's precisely these values and virtues that we celebrate at Christmas.

It doesn't actually matter that the words of the carols we sing are often sentimental, or talk about a world that no-one lives in any more (if indeed they *ever* did), a world of 'angels bending near the earth, to touch their harps of gold'. The reality is, of course, that the world does not (and never did) 'in solemn stillness lay/to hear the angels sing'. But you'd have to be a bit simple to think that the carol is giving us a bit of history. Rather, it's a word-picture of love, a way of expressing awe and wonder, and the deeply held conviction or feeling (and feelings are much more important on this occasion than facts) that love is the ultimate reality; that love matters; that love is the way forward; that a world in which love is dominant will be a much better place to live in than one in which fear and hate and greed and selfishness are the driving forces.

Christmas is an occasion when huge numbers of people really do take faith seriously, in that we really do try to be a bit more giving, a bit kinder, a bit nicer in general, than we usually are. Faith isn't about believing lots of unbelievable things, but about choosing to live in a particular way, daring to take certain values seriously. So when we take Christmas seriously (in other words, when we really do make an effort to be better people) we're doing so on the basis of faith; we're trying to put certain ideals into practice. To say 'yes' to the Christian faith is about saying yes to the example of Jesus: it's about trying to follow the lead that he gave, and the example that he provided. It's as simple (and as hard) as that!

Many churches are overflowing at Christmas, with about 40% of the population going to a carol service. Some 25% of people go to church on either Christmas Eve or Christmas Day, and this is about the same number as attend a pantomime. But whereas a pantomime is a bit of harmless escapism, an opportunity to get away from reality, religion should lead us further *into* life, by forcing us to take seriously the things that really matter. The theological term for what happened at Christmas is 'Incarnation', and is a way of trying to make sense of the idea that in the baby Jesus, God somehow 'came to Earth'. This raises all sorts of questions but the central point is clear enough: namely, if at the heart of Christianity there really *is* a God of Love (in other words, if Love is the value that we really *do* think is the most important thing in the world, and that we really *do* want to base our lives upon it) then it means that Love must also be at the heart of Christmas. Which is why the general bonhomie that's around at Christmas isn't just an add-on, but the very heart of the matter. And all the stories and the carols and the parties and the presents are aspects of this central truth.

There's no doubt that God is pretty irrelevant to most people in our society, in the sense that they rarely give him a thought. At Christmas he may get a bit of a look-in, and then it's back to normal. But this is largely the result of an enormous misunderstanding: God isn't one more thing among lots of other things. To 'think about God' isn't to think about some vast 'thing' – but about <u>every</u> thing. The reason why God seems so ludicrous to many people is because they've got an understanding that doesn't work for them. The solution isn't to ditch the idea of God, but to find an understanding that *does* work.

To ask questions about the sort of meaning that life can (and should) have, is to ask the most profound questions that there are. In other words, it's to ask *religious* questions – because 'religion' is the label we give to the attempt to wrestle with the most serious concerns that face humans beings. Many people find it helpful to think of God as a sort of invisible person, but lots of others find such an image a stumbling block. So why not take it all metaphorically instead? To be a Christian, a person obviously needs to take the Christian stories seriously, but that doesn't have to entail taking them *literally*! What matters is not what images or ideas are swimming round inside our heads, but the way those stories affect what we do, the way we live, the way we treat one another.

If you've ever tried pointing out something to a dog, you'll know that it looks at your hand, rather than at the thing you're pointing to. It's not its fault: dogs aren't that bright! In a similar way, the Christmas stories are ways of pointing to something profound, something beyond words. To focus on whether or not there really *were* choirs of angels or *how* the star wandered around the sky is to be like the dog, and miss the point! Religion can easily stay an affair of the head rather than the heart, and we need to let go and reach out. We need to celebrate and immerse ourselves in the joy and the beauty and the wonder of the world, just as we need to rage at the injustice and the cruelty and the oppression of the world. And if we really *do* want to make it a better place, taking the Christmas stories seriously is about as good a way as any to get started.

Chapter 11

THINKING ABOUT EASTER

Easter is a time when the loss of theological innocence (see Chapter 37) is felt very keenly by many people within the Church together with many of those outside as well. For them the rot set in when David Jenkins became Bishop of Durham in 1984. Even before his consecration he was in the headlines for the way he played down the significance of the physical aspects of the Resurrection. He was a symbol of hope for liberals and those on the edge of the Church, but rapidly became a hate figure for religious conservatives, the tabloid press and some members of the general public.

The irony was that none of the views he expressed were new: they'd all been around for well over a century and every theological college student would have had to think long and hard about them before being ordained. The way the press presented the story, however, gave the impression that the bishop had dreamed them all up himself, probably wilfully and spitefully in order to try and undermine the 'simple faith' of the 'simple believers'. Obviously there will be Christians who *are* simple, and it's good that they are a welcomed and valuable part of the Christian community. But it would be a travesty to suggest that 'the simple' made up the bulk of church congregations. And this means that the 'non-simple' need to be treated as adults by respecting their intelligence, rather than pretending that they have not advanced beyond the understanding of the early years in Sunday School.

The conservatives never forgave David Jenkins for daring people to try and take their faith with real seriousness by unhooking it from the shackles of literalness and exploring its spiritual aspects. This was scary for those who found thinking a challenge, and it was troubling for those who had a profound psychological need of certainty. It seemed that the Church had a disproportionate number of such people, and the noise they made was the result of genuine pain and upset. But there were many others who found that the invitation to look at religion in general, and the Resurrection in particular, in a spiritual way, was irresistible. It meant that considerable numbers of those who normally went nowhere near a church began to think about what Easter might mean when thought about in a grown-up way.

In terms of evangelism Easter is absolutely crucial, because without it there would never have been such a thing as Christianity. The Resurrection isn't simply another of the interesting events of the New Testament: it is the *foundation* of the New Testament, and to see it as just another member of the series of events centred on Jesus is to make what philosophers call a 'category mistake'. The Resurrection is the bottom-line for Christianity, it's what everything rests on: and like all bottom-lines, by definition there's nothing underneath to support *it*.

The Resurrection is what gave birth to the Church, to the Gospels, indeed to everything that makes up Christianity. But, more important than any of that, it's what keeps it all going today! Not because we see things in the same way that people did then, but because whatever it was that started it off is still around today. The story isn't conclusive, of course, and there are many intelligent, thinking people who find it all a lot of nonsense. Not because they're wicked or wilful, but because they are who they are.

For some people, though, the Resurrection is incredibly straightforward: Jesus came back to life, and simply walked out of the tomb. End of problem: you either believe it or not, but that's how it is!

Those who find that idea simply barmy tend to write off the whole of Christianity as well; whilst those who *are* able to take it literally tend to see it as a sort of test case: if you *can* accept it at face value, then you're a proper Christian; and if you *can't*, then you're not really terribly welcome until you can.

But maybe both groups are looking for the wrong sort of thing, and in the wrong sort of place. Resurrection can perhaps best be approached obliquely, in the way that Jesus used to do with regards to all sorts of things. For example, instead of focusing on its historical aspects, we might think about the way that writers, painters and poets try to express the reality of falling in love. If it's to be a good picture it has to bring home the fact that 'falling head over heels in love' involves a *total* change of perspective: to fall *head over heels* is to see things from a completely different point of view. And this is what the Gospel writers were trying to do when they wrote their Resurrection accounts.

They were trying to give some flavour of how the world had completely and utterly changed for those first disciples. To believe in the Resurrection does not require people to accept this, that, or the other reconstruction of what happened to Jesus on the first Easter Sunday. Such stuff exists only in the realms of speculation, and people can't be *expected* to base their lives on that – although undoubtedly many manage to do so. Resurrection is not a matter of speculation, but an explosion of meaning, as well as an invitation to share it. The meaning is the realisation that the Way of the Cross was not the *prelude to victory*, but the *Way of Victory itself.* It was (and remains) the realisation that the only power worth having is the power to do good, and the commitment to trying to live in and through this power. Most people, of course remain unconvinced, but that's not surprising. The pull of the self is so strong that the majority of people, sadly, can't escape its clutches.

It's ludicrous to think that what makes Christians Christians is the intellectual acceptance of certain propositions. Rather, it's the embracing of a vision, accepting the invitation to an adventure, to a way of living and dying that is worth bothering with. The proof of the pudding is always in the eating, and the Gospels bear witness to the fact that a group of beaten, dejected men and women were somehow, in some way, transformed by something into bold proclaimers of precisely this vision. We can't know what that 'something' was, but it was obviously sufficient to open their eyes so that they came to see Jesus' life and death as a victory and not a defeat. It gave them a new window on the world, because it showed that the power of love cannot be overcome. If God really is love (and it's surely impossible to be a Christian and not accept this) then the Resurrection is the story of that love being poured out into the world.

Unless the vision still 'worked', unless the reality underlying the Resurrection was still alive and well, Christianity would have died out long ago. But the fact that it didn't shows that the love and the joy and the hope and the peace that those first disciples felt had been unleashed into and on to the world is a force still very much to be reckoned with. But this will only be actualised if we make it happen; it's our responsibility to keep the reality of Resurrection alive. If we say 'Christ is risen', and then continue to be petty and backbiting and narrow and judgemental and gossipy and critical and generally nasty, we're showing loudly and clearly that it hasn't got a lot to recommend it. If, on the other hand, we find the whole idea mind-blowingly special and splendid, then that is bound to overflow into our lives, and we're going to be walking, talking, living and loving advertisements for Resurrection life.

It's this that enables us to break out of the tomb of despair; it's what enables us to overcome obstacles that threaten to grind us down; it's what enables us to enjoy life in its deepest and richest sense. You don't need any tests of doctrinal correctness: you simply need to look at people to see if they're still in the tomb of fear and timidity and selfishness and self-absorption, or whether they've escaped. It's not a once-and-for-all thing, of course: we tend to oscillate, sometimes inside the tomb, sometimes outside; but to have faith in the Resurrection means knowing that even when we're inside, we don't have to stay there.

The reason why so many people have problems with the Resurrection is that they refuse to take seriously the difference between the physical and the spiritual dimensions of reality. In fact, much of the time even those of us who take religion seriously may fail to do this, and act as if we believe that only physical things can be real, with spiritual things being thought of as very much second-class, really just a poor substitute because the genuine article isn't available. But of course orthodox Christian understanding is that it is the 'spiritual' that is really important because it is this that constitutes our divine aspect. What is truly real and important about us is our personality rather than our body, the latter being simply our physical expression rather than our essence. Whilst Open Christians would have all sorts of problems with such an understanding it does at least show that there is nothing new or controversial about taking the Resurrection in a spiritual sense.

The earliest and therefore perhaps the most authentic account of the Resurrection was that told by St Paul, and he says absolutely nothing about what happened to Jesus' body: for him the emphasis is solely on Jesus' 'spiritual body'. And whatever *this* is, it's not something that can readily be put into words. To talk of the Resurrection as 'a spiritual event', or of the post-Crucifixion appearances as 'spiritual experiences', is not to *explain* anything, but to say that here is something profound, something beyond anything we can make sense of. *To talk of a spiritual body is not to talk of a rather odd sort of body: it is to point to a mystery.*

The importance of this has long been recognised within Christianity by its ancient tradition of mysticism, and we need to try and recover something of this. Mysticism is the recognition that silence (see Chapter 25) and paradox may be the most appropriate responses to the Mystery-that-is-God, and sees the attempt to pin things down in straightforward terms as foolish and misguided, perhaps even idolatrous (see Chapter 27). The only sensible assumptions to make are that reality is always a lot more complex and interesting and profoundly wonderful than it looks, and there is always more than one way of exploring and expressing our beliefs. The fact that such assumptions are *still* not seen as self-evident shows what a long way there is to go.

Chapter 12

THINKING ABOUT MIRACLES

What are miracles? Do they happen? How can we tell? Do they matter? Some see miracles as *proving* the existence of God ('the occurrence of miracles shows that God's hands are at work'), whilst others see them as *presupposing* the existence of God ('if there is no God then there can be no such things as miracles').

For some people miracles are *doorways* to God, in that they provide them with reason for belief. Others, however, find them *obstacles*, in that they simply can't get their minds around them, and come to the conclusion that if this is the sort of thing that Christianity is about, then it's clearly not for them. A miracle is by definition an extraordinary event, but not just that: a trick done by a magician doesn't count. It also has to have 'religious significance', in that it results in believers seeing things differently, and may change unbelievers into believers. Miracles are, in other words, 'charged events' which make a difference to human lives afterwards. If a believer and an unbeliever witness the same extraordinary event, the believer may see it as a miracle, whilst the unbeliever may (and in fact is *bound* to, if he is to remain an unbeliever) simply see it as something very odd. Whose view is correct?

Miracles are events that cannot be explained, but they are not value neutral. If all of your friends died inexplicably one night, you

73

would rightly regard this as something very terrible. But if all of the people you disliked (and who, let us assume, were engaged in a plot to kill you) died inexplicably one night, you might be tempted to regard *this* as a miracle. Miracles have good consequences – at least from the point of view of the miracle-ascriber. In Exodus we read of how the waters of the Red Sea parted to allow the fleeing Israelites to pass through in safety, but then closed over (and drowned) the pursuing Egyptians. We may think of this event/story as a miracle, and this was certainly how the Israelites regarded it. But the widows and children of those Egyptian soldiers would presumably have seen things differently. Whose view is correct?

The point being made is that to call an event a miracle is not to label it in any normal way. It is to say that such an event is bizarre, perhaps frightening. It is not simply to say that we can't understand it: it's to say that we could *never* understand it. If, one day, an event that had traditionally been seen as a miracle was explained and thereby understood, the event, by definition, would cease to be a miracle – and we would have to say that what we once took to be a miracle was in fact something else. Miracles are logically connected to the notion of divine intervention – although that in itself is a problematic concept. Without a theistic God there could be no such thing as a miracle, at least as understood in the traditional way.

Miracle stories are common in many religious traditions, and Jesus' miracles, mainly healings, were a significant element in his ministry as recorded in the Gospels. Many people think that these 'healing miracles' are far more likely to have happened than the 'nature miracles', because there is plenty of evidence for psychosomatic illnesses, and hypnosis-type cures, whilst there is no evidence from our experience of the world to suggest that people can control nature by commanding it. The problem is that if this really is what happened, then in terms of the usual definition, such events don't actually *count* as miracles at all!

Belief in miracles is still strong, perhaps especially so amongst the ignorant and superstitious. It is always difficult to know what to make of reports of extraordinary events. As a general rule, the more improbable the claim, the more unreliable the supposed witnesses, the further back in time or the more remote in location is the event in question, the more evidence is needed and the more cautious we need to be. It is obviously not a coincidence that supernatural events appear to occur with greater frequency the further back in history we go. Each of us occupies our own particular position on the continuum that ranges from extreme scepticism to extreme gullibility. We don't choose where we are on the continuum: our position reflects the sort of person that we are, and indeed may change over time as we ourselves change. Some people, therefore, are more predisposed to believe in miracles (and indeed all sorts of other religious claims) than others, but religion must never be allowed to become their sole preserve.

A miracle, as traditionally understood, is an event that makes no sense: if it *does* make sense, it is not (and cannot be) a miracle. The disproof of a miracle would occur if the cause of the event in question could be discovered. An event is a miracle, not simply because it is extraordinary, but because it is *an event without a cause*. It's not a matter of having to establish *both* that there was no natural cause, *and* that God caused it: it's because it is believed that no identifiable causal agent is responsible for the event that it is said that God is responsible for it. But given that miracles seem to require the existence of an interventionist God, there is the very real question as to why God only works miracles for isolated individuals but didn't intervene to stop the monstrous evils wrought on millions of innocent people by Hitler and Stalin. Why are miracles usually *so small-scale?* And why does God apparently heal some people and not others? It's all terribly problematic!

Many people have difficulties with the miracle stories, not just of Jesus but elsewhere in the Bible as well. It's important that such difficulties aren't allowed to get in the way of faith, and there are various strategies for dealing with them. The first is simply to ignore miracles altogether. It is perfectly possible to take Christianity completely seriously and try to live by Christ's teachings whilst having nothing to do with any of the miracle stories. Doing this doesn't make someone less of a Christian, simply one who can live on rather thinner gruel than others seem to need. Another possibility is to rationalise the miracles, that is 'explain them away'. Each of the supposed miracles can be accounted for in some non-miraculous way, and such explanations can certainly help those who find them obstacles. The third strategy is to take them at face value. This doesn't mean to read them as historical or scientific accounts, but as attempts to convey a sense of awe and wonder, which was undoubtedly what those who told the stories were trying to do. Some of the miracle stories may be exaggerated, or even completely legendary, but this doesn't matter. Christians across the centuries have revered them, not because of what happened, but because of what they *mean*. Understanding them in this way means that they may cease to be obstacles and instead become doorways to the sacred.

It is in this sense that a baby may be described as a miracle: something that takes our breath away. Of course it may not: someone may simply say that a baby is a baby, and there's no big deal! But this brings out the important point that miracles are never unambiguous: they never provide knock-down arguments to *prove* anything. The Gospel accounts show that whatever Jesus did, there were many people who remained completely unmoved. In one sense they saw the same things as those who were *extremely* moved. But in another, much more important sense, they saw something *different* – or, rather, they saw very much *less*. The essence of the miraculous is not to be found in the event itself, but in one's *reaction* to the event. To say that something is/was a miracle is not to describe it, but to kneel before it.

Given such an understanding there can be no doubt that miracles *do* occur. People really *have* changed the direction of their lives in response to particular events (their first baby, the stillness of a mountain top, the selfless love of a relative) such that they *have* become more open and loving and generous. There may have been nothing particularly unusual in the events themselves, in that others may have barely noticed them at all, but despite this they acted as the trigger for a new way of seeing and (more importantly) being. We might go further and say that the truly miraculous is being able to find such meaning in amongst the ordinary, being able to move, as it were, to a different level of reality. Such 'moments of disclosure' are what 'finding God' amounts to.

Miracles always lead somewhere; they always take us forward in our spiritual journeying. It follows that we must be on the lookout for the miraculous, open to new sources of wonder and awe, ready to have our breath taken away from us. Our world is so glorious, so holy, so brimming with meaning, that it would be surprising if the miraculous were *not* all around us: our task is to be alive and alert to it, and to be prepared to live to the full whatever vision is granted us.

Chapter 13

THINKING ABOUT DEATH

Death is very much a taboo subject in our society: the young don't think about it because it's not sufficiently imminent, whilst the old tend to find it too scary to think about. There's often a sense of surprise on the part of many people when someone elderly they know dies: there shouldn't be, as this is simply the way the world works. But it's all part of the widespread denial about death. This often shows itself in the fact that as someone nears the point of death, people play a game of 'let's pretend', and talk about arrangements for when the person 'comes home'. Some deaths occur far too slowly, so that instead of death being an event it is a long drawn-out process of attenuation and diminution of the loved one. Such deaths also come far too late, in that long after any reasonable definition of worthwhile life has gone, the person continues in what is in effect a state of suspended animation, neither fully dead nor fully alive.

Faced with the death of a loved one, people may ask 'why did he have to die?' and this is an understandable, but misguided question. The person died because he was knocked down by a car, or because he had a heart attack, or because he caught typhoid or whatever. The cause of death is what is shown on the death certificate: all the facts are there. To ask, *in addition*, why he had the heart attack in the first place requires a working back through the causal chain, with considerations such as his diet, the amount of exercise he took, his family history and so on. But of course that's not what is being asked. What the man's wife or son are really saying is that they wish, more than anything in all the world, that he hadn't died; they're lamenting the way things have turned out. And their protests at the way they *have* turned out may lead them to the idea that everything that happens is part of some vast plan. If this *is* the case, of course, it makes perfect sense to ask why this particular feature was put in. Further reflection, however, may lead them to conclude that there is no reason to think that such a plan existed in the first place.

To ask 'why did it have to happen to me?' is equally senseless. There's no 'have to' about it: it just did. The principle of Ockham's Razor (see Chapter 31) leads us to adopt a cock-up rather than a conspiracy theory of history, and the same applies to everyday life. There's no *need* to look for hidden meanings and plans: and indeed trying to do so can suggest a planner (God) with some pretty alarming features, as is shown by the Problem of Evil (see Chapter 31).

Death is so final, so complete a break in the world of relationships, that in the face of it we can feel numb, and indeed if we think too much about it we may become seriously depressed. But the universality of death means that it has, somehow, to be confronted. Sometimes a death is seen as a relief because the person concerned was in so much pain that no one could have wanted him to continue like that. Sometimes a death may be a relief for the tragic reason that the person was widely loathed, and those around couldn't wait to be rid of him.

Most deaths, however, are sad affairs, and the funeral service (see Chapter 9) is a way of expressing and dealing with people's sense of grief. Christians are prone to feelings of guilt about all sorts of things, and death is no exception. It's sometimes said that the belief in eternal life should mean that funerals ought to be jolly occasions, but besides resting completely on the assumption of a particular eschatological outcome, such a view also fails to deal with the pain of parting. If I happened to be convinced that my wife was having a merry time in say, Australia, that wouldn't help take away the loneliness I was feeling here and now, loneliness which would be made a million times worse if I also knew that she was never coming home, and that I would never see her again. Even if someone subscribes to the idea of eternal life (see Chapter 35) there is no reason for them to assume that such a thing is *bound* to be, in some sense, simply a continuation of this life: it may be, but equally it may not. And if it isn't, then the notion of meeting up again with loved ones becomes almost impossibly problematic.

People feel so helpless in the face of death, and although there's an inevitability about this, given that there's nothing anyone can do to reverse the process, the sense of helplessness didn't used to be quite as pronounced as it is today. In earlier times there were all sorts of practical, hands-on ways in which people were involved. Family and friends would have washed and dressed the body, dug the grave, borne the coffin into church, and so on, but now it's all left to the professionals. They generally do a good job, but the result is that those close to the deceased can feel completely disempowered and excluded from it all.

Religion is a quest for seriousness and meaning, and as such is an ongoing attempt to help people *not* to duck the really profound and painful questions of life. This is why it's when people are really up against it, when they're completely at their wits end, that religion can come into its own, by providing them with a framework and a language for the serious reflection about personal priorities that everyone really ought to be constantly involved in. Do I get over-concerned about trivia? Do I value those around me enough? Do I make the most of every single second?

It might not be until the moment in the funeral service when the words 'earth to earth, ashes to ashes, dust to dust' are heard that the reality of all this fully hits home. They are spoken as the coffin is lowered into the ground, or as the crematorium curtains close, and are so solemn, so gut-wrenching, that they may bring to the surface the tears which up to that point have been kept under control. This moment of the funeral service throws everything into stark relief; but all too often the opportunity to confront the unknown is missed, and people retreat rapidly and gratefully back into the banal familiarity of the everyday. One of the things about religion, and the reason why many people find it too scary, is that it won't easily allow us to do this.

In St John's Gospel, Jesus talks about his death in terms of 'going away'. Thomas, one of the disciples, says 'Lord, we do not know where you are going', and that seems a pretty fair summary of the way most people think about death. It *is* an enormous mystery; it *is* an awesome unknown. Death is often seen as the great destroyer, and can threaten to embrace and destroy not just the dead but the living as well. This is because its existence can cast a long shadow over everything, despite the fact that it is the most natural and normal thing in the world. The faith of the Church is that the death and Resurrection of Christ have given us hope for the future; that death has lost its sting, and the grave has been denied its victory; that after death there is life. For many people this is a meaningless claim, and so it's important for those professionals trying to help the bereaved to find ways to reach them as well. The key thing is trying to focus on the triumph of hope over despair. In the midst of life there is death, and it's a very real and inescapable part of our world. But the Christian message of hope is that death does not have to have (and must not be *allowed* to have) the last word: despite the sorrow which death brings, new life is almost always available if people know where to look. The problem, of course, is that it isn't all to be found in the same place: each person needs to go on their own search for it.

Grieving is a process that begins with death, and should end with life, in that it is a journey that helps people to find a way of re-joining the everyday world. Not by denying the reality and finality of death, but by recognising that it isn't the end of the story. For some people though, it is: the death of a loved one brings their whole world crashing down, and they are unable to find a way out of the pit into which their grief has cast them. There is no formula that can help, and all that those around can do is support them as best they can.

Richard Holloway likens religion to sitting in a chair and looking into the distance. Doing this can be unsettling though, because of the sorts of things we see. Religious people are all too ready to rush in and instead of sitting alongside us and comparing notes, try to convince us that our view is wrong: there aren't really any scary things at all. Death is a case in point. Most people's view of it is so upsetting to them that they simply look the other way. Others manage to take comfort in the view that has seemed convincing to many across the centuries and has become a standard perspective of the Church. Still others, very much a minority, refuse to disbelieve the evidence of their own eyes, and manage to keep looking; and looking; and wondering.

Chapter 14

THINKING ABOUT THE SOUL

When I was about five our dog died. I asked what had happened to him and was told, not unreasonably, that he was in heaven. It's the sort of question that children ask, and it's the sort of answer that adults give them. But whilst this may work well enough when we're young, as we grow up the chances are we'll find such an answer less convincing. So where do animals go when they die? Do they, in fact, go anywhere at all? Perhaps they simply cease to exist? Pressing matters for someone whose much-loved pet has just died, and which raise the question as to whether animals have souls. This is difficult to answer, not least because it's not at all clear what a soul actually is. But the question that troubles most of us is not do animals have souls, but do humans have souls? If so, what sorts of things are they? And how can we find out?

To many people it seems to be self-evident that we're made up of three distinct things: physical stuff (the body), mental stuff (the mind) and spiritual stuff (the soul).

Human beings are seen as a mixture of these, which in some mysteroius way interact with each other. The physical bit, the body, is relatively straightforward, but the rest is a puzzle. Mind, soul, spirit and self occupy roughly the same sort of linguistic territory, and do roughly the same sort of job – although calling someone 'mindless' is very different to calling them 'soulless', just as saying that someone is very spiritual is different from saying that they are very soulful. All of these terms refer to our 'inner life', but their meanings are fluid, and different people may mean different things when they use the same words.

Human beings are *sentient* beings (we have sensations of various sorts), and we are also *self-conscious* beings (we are *aware* that we have sensations). This means that we have the capacity to reflect on our experiences, something that may be unique to us (and if not, is only shared with only a very few higher mammals). But what is it that *does* such reflecting? We are used to the idea that for things to happen there must be appropriate machinery: walking needs legs, eating needs a mouth, and so on. The conclusion that many people draw from this is that reasoning/thinking (of which reflecting is a part) needs a mind: in other words, there is a 'thing', *the mind,* 'inside' us, which carries out such mental operations. As the control centre for the body, people usually think of the mind as being located, somehow, in the brain.

Of course we're also *moral* beings (we have notions of right and wrong) and by implication this requires its own sort of machinery as well. If the reasoning takes place in the mind, our 'ethical supervision' presumably takes place somewhere *else*: perhaps the soul? This suggests a sort of internal hierarchy (a bit like the civil service with its clerical, executive, and administrative grades). At the lowest level is the body, subject to the directions of the mind; at the next level is the mind, subject to the directions of the soul, which as the initiator of everything, is at the summit.

Such a picture may or may not convince, but it doesn't really matter because it's *simply* a picture, and cannot be shown to be true (or false). The reason why we conjure up such pictures, or tell stories, is because we're such complicated creatures, that we need all the help we can get when trying to make sense of ourselves. We want to know what (if anything) is going to happen to us when we die; we want to know how we ought to live our lives; we want to know whether we really *are* special, or simply a sort of cosmic accident. We want to know all these things, together with many others – and are dismayed to discover that no one has the answers! There are plenty of suggestions around, of course, but no one can claim with any degree of convincingness really to *know*. Which is why the questions go round and round, from one generation to the next – and why people, in their desperation to know, are prone to clutch at religious straws of one sort or another.

When we talk about the mind it's easy to forget just what an odd thing we're doing. We have all sorts of mind-expressions, such as 'mind over matter', 'it's all in the mind', 'change your mind', 'call to mind' and so on. As a result, many people assume that the mind is a sort of ghostly object, which processes thoughts and stores memories. The principle of Ockham's Razor (see Chapter 31) suggests that it's probably safer to assume that the mind isn't a 'thing' at all, but rather a way of talking. In the same way, a lot of people find the conventional 'picture' of the soul simply incredible, but if they were to think of it as 'a way of talking', perhaps it would help them take it seriously in a way that they simply *can't* do at the moment?

There's an urgency about soul-questions that doesn't apply to mind-questions. This is because people's views about the soul are rarely disinterested, in that belief in the reality of the soul is usually linked to belief in life after death. To deny the existence of the soul is tantamount for many people to losing any hope of continuing the other side of the grave. But there's never any reason to suppose that truth and self-interest should coincide, and if we really want the former, we need to put the latter to one side.

'Do people have souls?' is a very different sort of question to 'do people have pineal glands?' No empirical evidence is needed (or indeed possible) to establish the answer, because it isn't that sort of question. We may say that Fred 'bared his soul to me', and this means not that he showed me some ghostly, intangible 'thing', but that he was unusually frank and open. A person's soul can thus be understood as the person-without-pretence, the person-without-masks. If we say of someone that he has no soul, we mean that he's cold and unfeeling, that he's not interested in other people –and *this* means that he's unable to be a full human being. Questions about the state of someone's soul, are not like questions about the state of his garden or his shoes – but about the sort of life that he's living: 'for what shall it profit a man, if he shall gain the whole world, and lose his own soul?' (Mark 8: 36) To lose one's soul is to lose everything that's worth having, it's to live without integrity, it's to be callous or shallow, it's to fail to take other people seriously: it's to fail to love.

'Soul-language' is the way we indicate the worth and value of a person. Perhaps it's not that 'having a soul' makes us morally special compared with the rest of creation: rather, it's *because* people are uniquely precious that we need (and use) soul-language in the first place. We have to have some way of bringing out the specialness of people, and 'soul-language' is the best we can do. But just as we talk about human worth or dignity, without assuming that there is some sort of substance or thing to which the words 'worth' and 'dignity' correspond, so we can also talk about the soul without having to make particular ontological assumptions about it. We might talk about someone feeling something 'in the depths of his heart' – or 'in the depths of his soul': both heart and soul are frequently used to refer to the 'essence' of a person, and the soul is also used interchangeably with the self.

The only reasonable way of approaching Reality is to assume that it is far more complex and mysterious and indeed wonderful than we think, and this means that anything we say about what it's like must be tempered with a great deal of humility. Perhaps the soul really *is* the ghostly thing that many people assume it to be, but it's probably better to work on the assumption that the whole question is a lot more profound and mysterious than such an approach suggests, which means that other ways of thinking about it need to be taken seriously.

We mustn't allow our faith to be imprisoned by literalism. Our language is so rich, and our use of it is so creative and imaginative that it would be boorish and stultifying to fail to recognise all the possibilities it gives us. If we say of someone that he's a 'man of spirit', we're not referring to some ghostly feature that he has, but to the fact that he's full of life, bursting with ideas and possibilities. In the same sort of way, if we say of someone that 'he'd sell his soul for money', we're not talking literally: it's not a matter of parting with some 'substance' in exchange for bank notes. We mean that he's got no integrity, that he's a shallow sort of person, that his life lacks adequate moral principles.

Some years ago in Britain the Militant Tendency infiltrated the Labour Party and threatened to make it unelectable, as a result of their extreme views and inflexible approach. Within Christianity there is a similar Tendency, at least as extreme and perhaps even more inflexible. Because their narrow and blinkered approach threatens to make Christianity impossible for thoughtful people, they might perhaps be termed the Philistine Tendency. They seem to be everywhere, and given the chance they will use the dead hand of ignorant, unimaginative literalism to squeeze the life out of soul-language, and indeed out of the rest of religion as well – but only if the rest of us allow them to.

Chapter 15

THINKING ABOUT FAITH AND DOUBT

Once upon a time, many, many years ago, tales were told of a far distant land. Little was known about it, save for the occasional stories brought back by the few people who had actually visited the place (or at least had spoken to others who, allegedly, had been there). From what they said, a rough and ready map was put together. Inevitably it had many gaps, but over the years these were gradually (and imaginatively) filled in, somehow or other. Such creative cartography didn't really matter, provided that the people looking at the map realised how it had come about.

The Christian tradition is just such a map, and it's similarly important to remember the way in which it has been produced. Disaster may strike if someone assumes that the map is the result of detailed and accurate surveying, and uses it accordingly. They may end up wandering around hopelessly lost as they try to match the reality they see around them with what the map says *should* be there. If their commitment to the map is sufficiently great (and their grip on reality sufficiently tenuous) they might even conclude that there were a disturbing number of ways in which the world itself was wrong! And whilst some might say that such an attitude showed commendably great faith, others might point out that in fact it showed the map-users had completely and utterly misunderstood the whole point of a map, which is to help you find your way around, rather than to act as a benchmark for reality.

Christian map-users occupy a series of positions, with two groups marking opposite ends of the spectrum: those who rely completely on the map, and who are prepared to defend, to the death if necessary, its God-given accuracy; and those who take it as self-evident that the map is a completely human creation which needs to be understood accordingly, and supplemented with whatever other materials are to hand.

The map-users in each of these two groups (and indeed any in between) have no real say as to the position on the spectrum they occupy: it's simply a case of being drawn to wherever most closely reflects the way they see things. Once there, it's a matter of getting on with life as best they can, acting in accordance with the perspective they've been given – which is what faith is all about. Faith is essential to religion: it's what turns ideas into practice. Its essence is *commitment*; taking a risk; leaping into the dark.

For many people, beliefs come before faith, logically *and* chronologically: unless they were confident that their picture of Jesus was historically accurate, they would be unable to make the necessary personal commitment to following him, which is the essence of Christian faith. Others are able to make the leap of faith *without* a foundation of particular beliefs at all, or are able to hang on to faith even when the beliefs that had earlier seemed compelling do so no longer. For them, faith is not to do with propositional knowledge, but a matter of choosing a path that seems likely to lead to human flourishing. People may thus come to faith *because of* beliefs – or *in spite of* beliefs! Those in the former group may find it difficult to understand how the latter are able to do this, but however mysterious it is to them, the faith of the latter is as life-giving and robust as that of the former.

Two people may hold the same beliefs (in terms of agreeing about certain facts) but view things very differently. Much political debate is not disagreement about facts, but about visions. In the same way two people could each accept a series of propositions about Jesus and his teachings, but whilst one finds them a matter of indifference to the way he lives his life, the other tries to put them into practice.

Belief and faith can each give rise to doubt. I may find that one or more of my beliefs about the world has come to seem less persuasive than it once was, either as a result of further reflection, or as a result of coming across beliefs held by other people, which raise questions about my own position. Similarly, the way I see the world, the framework within which I try to make sense of things, may come to seem less satisfactory, and I may find myself unable to commit to it with the same level of enthusiasm. I may modify the framework, or even eventually abandon it altogether.

The latter, if referring to a religious perspective, is usually called 'losing one's faith', but this is misleading as it implies that 'faith' is something solid, something specific, rather than being the name we give to the ongoing struggle of human beings to make sense of their lives. If I fail to keep up the payments on my mortgage, I may 'lose my house', the place where I live; but however tempting it may be to compare this to 'losing my faith', the spiritual place where I live, if I fail to keep up my beliefs, it cannot be done. My house is an obvious entity, whereas my faith is the solid-sounding name given to the current perspective I have on the world, a perspective that is continually changing as a result of the dynamic interchange between myself and my surroundings.

Doubt occurs whenever a gap opens up between personal experience and the picture given by dogma or tradition or scripture – and where the former is taken sufficiently seriously so that the latter aren't seen as *automatically* having the last word. It occurs when we, so to speak, outgrow our intellectual or political or religious clothes: we may be able to put up with the resulting discomfort for a while, but if it becomes sufficiently painful we will be forced to have them altered, or in extreme cases, replaced altogether (going round without wearing any is not a realistic option). And although it's sometimes painful, doubt is always an invitation to move forwards, an opportunity to grow – and for that we should be thankful.

It is commonly thought that strong faith never doubts, and because strong faith sounds a lot more worthwhile than weak faith, it presumably follows that doubt is something we should be sad about – or even ashamed of. But what is meant by the term 'strong faith'? A way of looking at the world that is set in concrete? A way of looking at the world that can never change? Instead of being something laudable, this can easily become a fast track to fanaticism. We should hold on to our faith only for as long as it continues to help us grow in love, only for as long as it continues to feed our sense of awe and wonder.

Our faith, like our beliefs, needs to be kept constantly under review, measured in terms of our ethical principles. If our outlook ever becomes hard and intolerant and judgemental, then we'd be better off with a different perspective. Many Communists started off full of idealism, but ended up serving a regime of terror, and the Church can easily become an oppressor rather than a liberator. A 'strong faith' may mean a blinkered outlook, and therefore something that can do more harm than good. If it's doubt that makes the difference between a strong and a weak faith, given that it can be an invaluable antidote to the inanities and insanities that sometimes go on in the name of religion, we need more of it, not less.

People may be divided into those who see the teachings of Christianity as the religious equivalent of a detailed Ordnance Survey map, and those who see them more like crude scrawlings that show where the pirate's treasure is supposed to be buried. The former look to religion to provide the answers that quell doubts, whilst the latter see it as giving hints and possibilities which take those doubts seriously. Most thoughtful people accept that existential doubt is not a matter of being indecisive but of being open to new possibilities. Doubt helps to keep us humble, and is what drives us to explore and to grow. It's what spurs us into asking questions, and is the reason why religion and children often don't go well together. Children persist in asking questions, a practice that most adults have found is not encouraged in religion, and which they have therefore suppressed.

Question: 'Where did the world come from?'

Answer: 'God made it.'

Question: 'Who made God?'

Answer: 'That's enough questions!'

Children simply *won't* shut up, and adults who take religion seriously ought to learn some healthy doubt from them. We all need to be far more ready to ask questions and to refuse to be fobbed off with the cliché-ridden, jargon-laden theobabble that is all around us, and which threatens to wash away all intelligent debate in the Church.

Chapter 16

THINKING ABOUT RELIGIOUS QUESTIONS

Most people in our society have no interest in religion, just as they have no interest in stamp collecting or train spotting – all seen as eccentric but pretty harmless ways of spending one's time. There are various reasons why religion is generally not taken seriously, but one of the big stumbling blocks for many intelligent people is that religion seems to demand the suspension of common sense, and the inhabiting of a strange thought-world, where all sorts of bizarre things are taken for granted, and where asking questions is seen as rather bad form.

Religion can give people a sense of peace, but this may be because of the sense of certainty that often comes with it as well. This can make them deaf to new ideas or perspectives, and when religious *certainty* is combined with religious *zeal*, the result can be bigotry, persecution and violence. Things don't have to be like this, and perhaps the best way of helping to prevent religion getting out of hand is to try and keep it out of the ghetto-world into which it tends to retreat. And *this* is best done by making sure that those involved in it never stop asking questions. The problem is that thinking about religion is hard work, and requires a willingness to be open to new ideas.

Asking religious questions can make one unpopular, not least because lots of religious people see religion as their only anchor in an uncertain world, and cling on desperately to what they've got. Asking questions is often seen as dangerous – for the good reason that it often is! The numerical success of the Alpha courses shows that they meet a real need of very many people – a need for clear answers to the big questions of life. But there may well be even more who are repelled by what they see as its pre-packaged shallowness and superficiality, and who wouldn't dream of getting involved in a spiritual quest where the answers are claimed to be so readily available.

Religious questions, like all questions, are both expressions of ignorance and attempts to reduce it. They're asked in the hope of finding out what is the case, what is true. But as Pontius Pilate realised, it's one thing to have a vague interest in truth – and quite another to be passionately committed to searching for it. All too often we take the easy way out and content ourselves with second-hand answers, ones proffered by others. Some people are easy to please in this respect, and readily adopt other people's views and beliefs; others are more sceptical, and may look on with wonderment at the ease with which many are able to stop thinking about things, and achieve 'closure' of the issue. Conservative Christians tend to feel the need for closure, and cannot readily live with uncertainty, whereas liberals are more than able to cope with the 'openness' that unanswered questions brings.

Jesus said that he was the Way rather than the Answer. To see him as 'the Answer' would lead not to life but to death, because it would mark the end of the journey. The religion that grew up on the basis of his example and teachings shouldn't be seen as a set of answers but as a way of taking the issues of morality and mortality with the seriousness that they deserve. Being a Christian, therefore, is not a matter of having a particular set of answers, but of looking at the questions from a particular perspective.

It is very unfortunate that religion has become so widely identified with an attitude of unthinking acceptance of the ideas of other people, not least because many of those involved in religion give up their own search for truth as a result. Because the quest is an exhausting business, it's a lot easier to settle for off-the-peg religious opinions; but although many people seem to be able to wear such ready-made religious clothes, there are an awful lot more whom they *don't* fit – and indeed will *never* fit. At present, those who aren't, spiritually speaking, a standard size, are left high and dry; and this is because their attempts to ask searching questions are not taken seriously in the churches, which can't bear anyone to rock the boat. After all, some of the people on board might start feeling seasick as a result, and concern for *their* comfort seems to be paramount (and certainly a lot more important than trying to get people on board who are currently flapping around in the water).

Unless and until the needs of those currently *un*involved with the churches are taken seriously, the place of religion in educated societies will (rightly) continue to decline. Far from being the enemies of religion, those who ask searching questions of it are in fact the only hope that the churches may have of being be shaken out of a galloping irrelevance, and dragged, kicking and screaming, into the 20th century (it's probably best to be realistic about this, and not entertain serious hopes of a leap straight into the 21st century in one go).

Many people can make no sense of philosophy, and can't see why its questions are of any interest to anyone. Philosophers are still asking many of the same questions that were being asked well over 2000 years ago, and because this is taken to mean that no progress is possible, the whole enterprise is written off as pointless by the less reflective. It's a criticism that is also made of religion, whose concerns are even more similar to those of over 2000 years ago, whereas disciplines such as engineering or physics have long since answered the questions that bothered the Greeks, and are now addressing very different ones. But instead of showing the irrelevance of philosophy and religion, this simply indicates that the problems they are concerned with are of a completely separate order. Scientific problems have been termed 'convergent', because the more they are studied, the more the answers proposed tend to converge, until eventually agreement is reached, and the problem is said to be 'solved' – which means that as a problem it disappears. In contrast to this, the problems of philosophy and religion generally show no sign of convergence, and indeed the responses that people make to them may move further and further apart. They are said to be 'divergent' problems, and are characterised by the lack of acknowledged experts.

Of course, there are plenty of people who may think of themselves (or may be thought of by others) as experts, but their claims are unfounded. The practice (as opposed to the study) of religion is not an academic discipline like physics or history: it's not something that people can become more and more knowledgeable about. Instead it's much more like developing a relationship, which is something no one can do for you. As an academic discipline theology has its own authorities, but although they may be God-*talk* experts (knowing lots about what others have thought and said about God) this does not make them *God*-experts! Indeed, theologians are sometimes thought of as rather God-*less*, on the grounds that they are far too sceptical about the whole religious enterprise for many people's taste!

It may be a grave disappointment, perhaps even a shock to many churchgoers, but it isn't even possible to think of *bishops* as God-experts. Although they are often pleased to give *ex cathedra* rulings, and indeed are expected by many to pronounce with confident authority about all sorts of things, there is no reason whatsoever to suppose that they have been vouchsafed truths that are inaccessible to the rest of us. Their institutional role may oblige them to bring about closure of doctrinal disputes, but although this can help make the world seem a safe and ordered place, it is nothing other than a convenient ecclesiastical procedure. It would be preposterous for anyone to suggest that a genuine search for truth could ever be artificially terminated in this way – but it's a sad fact that in religion being preposterous is rarely seen as much of a stumbling block!

Chapter 17

THINKING ABOUT THEOLOGY

What does all this religious stuff *mean*? And is it *true*? These are the two most important questions that anyone can ask about religion; and this means that they are the two most important *theological* questions that there are, because theology is the enterprise that tries to make sense of religion. Most religious believers don't tend to see the point of such questions: for them, the practice of religion is enough. And for pretty well everyone else, the questions never arise at all.

This is all an enormous shame because the questions really do need asking! There are so many peculiar things said and done in church services that a casual visitor would be bound to wonder just what was going on. All sorts of odd claims are made, all sorts of odd words are used; there is just so much scope for nonsense being talked that there needs to be some way of distinguishing between the simply weird and the truly profound. This is part of what the branch of theology known as *philosophical* theology is *for*: to help us understand what religious claims amount to (when we talk about 'God the Father', what do we *mean*?) and to point out when they don't actually mean much at all: to help us say what we mean, and to remind us not to say more than we are entitled to.

Theology means, roughly, 'God-talk', and much of it involves *reflection on* God-talk, the examination of religious claims. Its results may provide doorways into religion, which makes it of vital importance to many of those who are outside the Church and unable to find a way in. Theology can thus help people into religion, and as such is like a bridge or a ladder. But once someone has got to where they want to get, they don't need the bridge or the ladder any more: they may have little use for theology afterwards. Theology can also, of course, be a way *out* of religion, in that reflection could lead people to the conclusion that the whole thing is nonsense. Because this is always a possibility, those whose faith is necessary for their psychological survival tend to steer well clear of it.

All the while that someone is happy with their religious practice there's no pressing need for them to have anything to do with theology, although it's probably a good idea to have some nodding acquaintance with it, in case problems arise in the future. It's a bit like art: someone might be perfectly happy simply visiting art galleries and looking at the paintings – until he comes across a style of painting that mystifies and disturbs him. It is then that he might feel the need to study the background of the painter, finding out who influenced her, what she 'means' by painting in this way, and so on.

There's something deeply depressing about the fact that in all other academic disciplines the search for truth is open-ended, whereas in theology, all too often, it is closed. In all other disciplines new insights are greeted with approbation, whereas in theology they are, all too often, greeted with hostility, fear and negativity. In all other disciplines there is a genuine sense of discovery, of venturing and exploring; whereas in theology the orthodox view is that the end-point is well known, and so it's only a matter of filling in the details. In all other disciplines the leaders are the pioneer thinkers, whereas in religion (the parent of theology) the bishops are the leaders, and they are the ones who often put a *brake* on thinking.

But far from being the enemy of religion, theology is essential to its health. It can help guard against arrogance, by reminding us how fragile are the religious positions we adopt. All theology (like all religion) is human, in that all God-talk (that is, talk *about* God) is talk *by* humans. It can't be anything else, of course, but it means that it's all tentative, it's all provisional – and it's all down to us. Theology is hard work, and requires a willingness to read, to think and to discuss. It also demands that we are open to new ideas, whereas lots of religious people see religion as their anchor in an uncertain world, and so cling on desperately to what they've got – ask too many questions and you might find that your anchor fails to hold.

Many religious claims look as if they're straight out of J.K Rowling's *Harry Potter*, who finds that if he runs hard enough at a wall he can get into a different dimension. In religion it's as if people think that provided we run hard enough at *language*, we will get through its barrier and enter a different sort of world. In fact we can all too easily end up with nonsense-on-stilts! But theology (and particularly *philosophical* theology) won't allow *any* religious claims to go unchallenged, which is why its practitioners are often regarded with such fear and hostility. The shakier the foundations, the more frightening people find it when theologians and philosophers start to probe away at the assumptions!

Those who are able to accept all sorts of extraordinary religious claims are sometimes said to be people of 'great faith', but in fact the opposite tends to be the case. They are the ones who find the challenges of theologians particularly threatening because they might undermine their whole world. The more fervently someone's faith is held, the more fragile and brittle it tends to be, and the more liable to fall to pieces at any moment. This is why it can be argued that it is the liberals/radicals (see Chapters 18 and 19) who are the ones of great faith: despite being only too well aware of how easily the whole thing might begin to unravel, they're prepared to hang on in there and risk everything as they keep asking questions.

There's no doubt that theology can be a thankless enterprise: it involves great effort, and it makes no promises. It certainly doesn't guarantee to give answers that are either comfortable or comforting. The questions it deals with are huge ones, questions that can't actually be 'answered' in the sense of bringing about closure. In fact they are more akin to questions about the Meaning of Life (see Chapter 36). The definitive spoof on that was given by Douglas Adams, in *The Hitch-Hiker's Guide to the Galaxy*, when he said 'the answer to the Great Question Of Life, the Universe and Everything ... Is ... Forty-two!' The very idea that there is an 'answer' to such questions is absurd. They are not normal questions, they're not like questions about what time the train goes or what is the boiling point of water; rather, they're a way of saying 'I don't know my way around'; they're saying that here is a mystery which we ought to ponder.

Theology can be scary and upsetting; taking it seriously can lead people to all sorts of unwelcome conclusions, and this applies as much (if not more) to the clergy as it does to the laity. Clergy who don't read and discuss theology might be compared to doctors who don't read the *British Medical Journal*; but whereas the latter would rightly be castigated, clergy who *do* read and discuss are likely to be seen as boat-rockers. Many people (including some bishops) seem to think that the main job of clergy is keeping the religious show on the road, by coming out with appropriate platitudes at all times and in all places. Far from it being seen as a good thing for clergy to encourage their congregations to explore the nature of faith, the important thing is to keep a lid on such notions! In the circumstances, and especially in the light of what happens to those who dare to follow arguments wherever they lead, it's not at all surprising that so little root and branch theological thinking is done within Church circles. Theology is seen as mainly a matter of filling in the gaps rather than raising genuinely unsettling questions.

The claims of religion often *look* as if they are factual, but when they are treated as such and questions asked about them, religious believers can get very defensive very quickly. Unless these believers learn to adopt a more open and mature attitude the future for organised religion in our society is bleak. What *can* most people make of a claim such as 'Jesus died for our sins and rose again'? What *can* someone do with the statement that in order to be 'saved' (and what might that mean?) someone needs to 'accept Jesus as Lord'? Religion is riddled with such stuff; words strung together to make religious mantras which are said over and over again. They become so familiar that people may barely think about them – until someone comes along and breaches religious etiquette by asking what on earth is going on.

Given the enormous chasm that exists between the Church and secular society it may be that theology is the only hope for religion. It's the job of theology to make sure that the difficult and unwelcome questions get asked, especially those asked by religious outsiders. Theology is perhaps the only thing that can act as a bridge between Church and society, but the task is mammoth. Dumbed-down religion is currently all the rage, with those churches that offer simple answers tending to attract much larger congregations than those which make greater intellectual demands on people. But in the longer term it seems likely that unless the Church takes theological thinking in particular, and critical thinking in general a lot more seriously it will need to prepare for its own extinction.

Chapter 18

THINKING ABOUT LIBERAL THEOLOGY

Theology is, literally, 'God-talk': an attempt to make sense of faith; an impossible attempt to understand the non-understandable. It's bound to fail, perhaps badly so. But it's important to be able to assess this God-talk, so that we can try to weed out the reasonable failures from the hopeless failures: we need some criteria, some concepts to help us. Like all concepts these are human inventions, in no way objective, and bound to favour certain perspectives more than others.

The hallmarks of liberal theology are (or at least should be) openness, humility, and lack of dogmatism. It is (or at least should be) pluralistic, because it accepts that our ignorance is so great that anything we say about God is bound to be tentative and provisional. Conservative Christians seem able to make sweeping statements about God with enormous confidence. From the liberal perspective such utterances are not seen as resulting from unusual insight, but from unusual stupidity.

Liberal theology is not something clear-cut, but a way of approaching theological questions. Inevitably it includes a great range of views, ranging from the relatively conservative to the truly radical. Their common feature, however, is the way they embrace rather than shy away from the modern world. Conservative religion tends to see threats all around, with religion being subject to a pincer movement of science and the arts, which between them exemplify the godlessness of our time. Liberal theology, on the other hand, accepts the need for theology to develop, and does not hanker after the past. It is always looking for ways in which the Gospel may be reinterpreted and proclaimed afresh. Liberals look for ways to affirm rather than criticise, to include rather than to exclude, to celebrate rather than to condemn. Charges of 'woolly liberalism' are frequently directed at the unwillingness of liberals to make a firm stand on anything, and is the inevitable accompaniment of being open. The classical liberal dilemma, whether of theology or politics, is how far it can tolerate the intolerance of the conservatives.

Liberal theology takes seriously the scientific worldview, and refuses to retreat into a religious ghetto where people who think alike gather together for mutual support. Instead, it looks for ways of integrating theology with developments in science and philosophy that do not insult people's intelligence. The liberals' approach to the Bible or to God reflects this position of open questioning. They play down the importance of 'facts' in theology, and instead set great store on myth and symbol, not seeing this position as in any way a problem or as something for which they ought to apologise.

Liberals are able to live with questions, a characteristic of many of those who have enjoyed the benefits of higher education. Their world is not black-and-white, but innumerable shades of grey. Living in the midst of Mystery, liberals never think that they can do anything more than (at best) scratch the surface of things. Neither do they think that they can take theology seriously without experiencing considerable tension: the liberal position is in the no-man's land between entrenched religious conservativism and secular humanism, and this is about as uncomfortable a place as it's possible to be. Rather than simply looking for ways of surviving in such hostile territory, liberals try to produce a synthesis out of the two perspectives.

Scientific progress occurs as a result of the identification of error, as new thinking shows ways in which earlier thinking was wrong, or at least limited in scope. Religious people sometimes say that this shows the superiority of theology, in that although scientists always seem to be changing their minds, theologians rarely do. Another way of looking at this, however, is to say it shows that theology is a closed system, and that theologians wear blinkers. Moving on, therefore, may be a sign of either strength or weakness, depending on one's perspective. Science operates on the basis of critical enquiry, and the willingness to subject all ideas to close and continual scrutiny. Nothing is off-limits, nothing is sacred.

Liberal theology used to be seen as an attempt to prevent secularism having the last word. Over recent centuries, scientific advances have completely transformed the way people look at the world, and have given many a sense of being in control. For most people in the prosperous parts of the world, religion has become a matter of almost complete irrelevance, with lives being lived without any reference to it whatsoever. People still had spiritual needs, of course, but these weren't being satisfied, and perhaps not even acknowledged by the people themselves. Liberal theology was an attempt to show how it was possible to combine a scientific view of the world with a thoughtful understanding of scripture, and produce a theology that did not insult people's intelligence.

Although many rejected this approach, with some arguing that it was undermining faith, and others that it was *still* a lot of nonsense, it undoubtedly succeeded in keeping faith alive for many educated people. But just as liberal theology was a response to the ways that 19th-century ideas were putting faith under pressure, so radical theology (see Chapter 19) is a response to the ways that 21st-century ideas are putting faith under pressure today. Occupying the space between religious conservatism (which is always in danger of spilling over into religious fundamentalism) and secularism (which is always in danger of spilling over into political fundamentalism) liberalism is used to being squeezed. Recent years have seen the pressure coming, not from secular agencies but from conservative religion, as the world becomes a more bigoted place, with rampant fundamentalisms of all sorts on the increase (see Chapter 28).

Anglicanism is often seen as a synthesis of reason, scripture and tradition, with an individual's own position reflecting the particular strength of these three 'forces', which might be thought of as being the three apexes of a triangle. Someone who finds reason particularly important will tend towards liberalism; someone who finds scripture particularly important will tend towards Evangelicalism; someone who finds tradition particularly important will tend towards Anglo Catholicism. The balance between these forces may change during a person's life, and if the pull of reason is overwhelming, the person may get dragged out of the triangle altogether, and abandon religion completely. And just as liberalism worked to show that the pull of secular reason need not mean that thoughtful people should leave the triangle, so it also needs to resist the pull of religious fundamentalism of all sorts as they try to drag people away from any contact with reason.

It is difficult (if not impossible!) to imagine circumstances in which there is too much reason in religion: the problem is far more likely to be its undervaluing, in relation to tradition and scripture. And although liberal theology emphasises the role of reason it is not a case of valuing *only* reason. Liberal biblical scholars have shown how the Bible can be understood intelligently and critically, whilst liberal catholics, in the Lux Mundi tradition, have shown how reason can inform (and be informed by) tradition.

Liberals try to be tolerant of other points of view, but the problem of what to do in the face of intolerance is very real. Other Christians can be so narrow and exclusive that it may be impossible to see their perspective as simply 'equal but different'. It's not a case of refusing to tolerate their intolerance, but of wanting to engage with it and try to open the matter up to discussion. Other faiths may be a much greater problem; in particular those that still have barbaric and sickening punishments for anyone judged to have stepped out of line. It would be Moral Relativism gone mad were liberals simply to go along with such behaviour out of a desire not to offend other people's sensitivities. There are times when basic human rights have to take precedence over everything else, and these must be for liberals the bottom line.

The openness of liberal theology is not the result of some peculiar generosity of spirit, but a reflection of the genuine desire of liberals to learn from the insights of others. If you already feel you know the answer before you engage in conversation, the interchange becomes simply an exercise in evangelistic drum-banging (see Chapter 26) rather than a real opportunity for both parties to learn and to grow. Liberal theology sees truth as much in the search as in the destination, which is why it attracts those who are always on the move. Perhaps its conservative critics need to get out more?

Chapter 19

THINKING ABOUT RADICAL THEOLOGY

Liberal theology (see Chapter 18) asks far more questions than most people in the Church are comfortable with: but it doesn't ask nearly enough for many of those outside. It might be compared with the state of physics at the beginning of the 20th century. The Newtonian system (see Chapter 37) had worked well enough for centuries, but was coming up against an increasing number of observations that simply didn't make sense when looked at in terms of the old framework. Honesty demanded that they were not ignored, but their existence was an increasing embarrassment. The result was a new framework, particularly associated with Einstein. It didn't show that the old framework was wrong; rather, it was of more limited application than the new framework. For most purposes Newtonian physics worked perfectly satisfactorily, but it was incapable of doing all that was being asked of it in the new situation.

In a similar way, the developments and modifications of orthodox Christianity associated with liberal theology have managed to accommodate most of the new ideas in science and other disciplines, and allowed theology to continue to speak to many of the questioning minds of our time. But increasing numbers of people found that liberal theology didn't go far enough, and unless substantially more far-reaching changes were made, they would be unable to continue engaging with religion. The result has been the development of the ideas of Radical Theology, associated with such figures as Don Cupitt, Richard Holloway and John Spong.

Cupitt has been particularly innovative and far-reaching in his thinking and, as a result, has been seen by many conservative Christians as a threat. He has written over 30 books, in the course of which his ideas have developed in all sorts of ways. This makes it almost impossible to characterise and summarise his theological views, but he is especially associated with the idea of 'non realism'. This rejects the idea that God is an 'object' or 'thing' of some sort, and instead sees him/her/it as a symbol capable of inspiring and guiding us. And while in one way this makes the whole theological enterprise different, in another, it leaves everything as it was. The practice of religion (hymns, Bible readings, prayers, and so on) continues as before, except that rather more people feel able to join in than would be the case if such an alternative way of understanding things didn't exist. Far from being a threat to Christianity, non realism is one way in which it can continue to speak to some of the people who would otherwise have left the Church altogether, or indeed not joined in the first place.

The radicals face the same problem the liberals had to face: namely, the narrowness and intolerance of many other Christians. But because the radical perspective is even further removed from that of conservative Christians, the hostility it provokes is even greater. Part of this is based on an inability to understand a different way of looking at things; and part is due to a lack of imagination, which means they cannot empathise with those for whom the traditional views are impossible. Some radicals have been guilty of a certain shrillness, giving the impression that only their perspective is valid; and although this is perhaps the mirror image of the conservatives, it is nevertheless regrettable. A radical who is genuinely pluralistic will see her perspective as only one of an unlimited number: if her way of looking at religion can *also* help other people, well and good, but she is unlikely to want to try and change the way they see things so long as they are willing to respect the perspectives of others.

One of the functions of the Bank of England is to act as 'lender of last resort' to the commercial banks. In the event of a cash shortage, the banks can approach it for assistance, but because it can name its own terms this is a step they would take only if all else failed. In a similar way, non realism might be thought of as a 'theology of last resort'. Those who can cope with orthodox religious beliefs have no reason to engage with non realism at all, and because of all the acrimony associated with it, would probably be advised to steer well clear. But increasing numbers of people are finding orthodox beliefs impossible, and for them the choice is very stark: having nothing to do with religion – or exploring radically different approaches, such as non realism. This doesn't mean that non realists should feel like second-class Christians: simply that people tend to end up as non realists *only* when they have found more conventional ways of thinking impossible.

Whereas liberal theology might be thought of as finding new ways of believing old things, radical theology is for those who argue that the modest tinkering of the liberals does not go far enough, because it *still* does not allow them to take religion seriously, *which is what they want to be able to do.* Instead of looking at the old things from a slightly different angle, the radicals have to reinterpret them drastically. Some would say that in doing this, the radicals are changing religious concepts out of all recognition, and so should stop using the same words. 'God' is the obvious example of the way this works: the traditional understanding of God is of an actual being, who 'exists' in some sense. The radicals don't find this helpful (even though it obviously does help, and has helped, hundreds of millions of people) and want to 'reinterpret' (that is, expand the meaning of) the idea of God so that it is understood as a symbol. Their critics respond that by doing this, the entire essence of

'God' has been destroyed, and nothing except obfuscation can be achieved by continuing to use the same word.

But the radicals aren't being intentionally awkward; neither are they wanting to legislate for others. What they are trying to do is find ways to enable *themselves* to continue taking religion seriously: what matters is putting religion into practice, trying to live your life on the basis of the teachings of Jesus. They would say that the details of the mental processes that go on inside people's heads, which allow you to go to church in the first place, are beside the point. The only important issue is the way in which going to church, with all that it entails, informs and inspires your daily living. Although belief is a major thing for religious traditionalists, for the radicals it doesn't tend to be. There are, of course, many things that the conservative Christian manages to believe that the radical can't, but there may well be many other things that the radical doesn't so much *dis*believe as feel unable to come to a decision about at all. What matters, to the radical, is the *praxis* of religion, the living-out of Christ's teachings, however understood.

Wittgenstein wrote that 'an honest religious thinker is like a tightrope walker. He almost looks as though he were walking on nothing but air. His support is the slenderest imaginable. And yet it really is possible to walk on it'. This brings out the point that non realism is never going to be of mass appeal: it's hard to understand it, and it's even harder to practise it. Many non realists feel the loss of the objective God very keenly: Cupitt wrote 'do not tell me that this complete loss of objectivity is hard, for nobody knows that better than I do'. And again, 'I have no wish to conceal the arduousness of this spiritual journey. I did not undertake it willingly, and I only venture to recommend it now because we have come to a time when it is the only recourse left to us.'

People laughed at Nietzsche's Madman, because he was looking so passionately for God, and was so obviously and painfully unable to find him in the conventional places – just as they *still* laugh at people who do this. Those outside the Church may see the whole spiritual question as absurd; whilst those inside may wonder what all the fuss is about, because surely everything is laid out in the Bible? The religious radical is therefore under fire from both camps, each of which is confident of the rightness of its own views. In the end, perhaps, wisdom lies simply in learning to live with question marks, comfortable in the company of those who see things differently.

Chapter 20

THINKING ABOUT ATHEISM

Most people in Britain are, in practical terms, atheists. They may profess some form of religious belief when asked by pollsters, but probably this is because there's a rather chilling finality about coming out as an atheist. Their lives are generally lived without any reference to religion: they don't go to church, they don't read or reflect on the Bible, they don't pray. In other words, they don't do any of the things that constitute religious behaviour. If this is pointed out they may get defensive and say things like 'you don't have to go to church to be a Christian', but they aren't able to indicate on what grounds they might count as one.

God may make a brief appearance in their lives at times of great personal crisis (bereavement, serious illness, impending death) but is otherwise absent. The Church, desperate for members, clings to the idea that such people have a 'religious sense', and so could be enticed along if only the services were made shorter or jollier, or the vicar was nicer, or whatever. But such strategies don't work – and never will: the Church needs to accept that most people in our society live atheistic lives, because unless it does, it will fail to engage with where they actually are.

Part of the problem, of course, is that Christianity seems to require people to believe the unbelievable and to endorse the incredible – miracles, life after death, a disembodied Supreme Being, and so on. Each of these seems so preposterous to so many people that there's no chance of them being accepted; and if that's the admission charge to Christianity, then they'll continue to walk on by. To a large extent, much of this is the fault of education, in that people are increasingly encouraged to think for themselves rather than simply accept what others say. And given that so much religion is based on what is claimed to be Divine Revelation or the ancient Authority of the Church, it's hardly surprising if this has led to most of it being rejected as ludicrous by many thinking people.

But although most people tend to live their lives without any reference to religion they cannot do the same with regard to ethics. Everyone has to have a moral code of some sort, and in the absence of religion the basis of those values may seem problematic. The loss of religion does not mean the loss (or rejection) of values, but if called upon to justify the basis of the values they hold, many people would find themselves at something of a loss. The contrast between the self-confident advance of science and technology, and the cultural pessimism and uncertainty within which such advances occur could hardly be greater. Western societies get richer and richer, but this is accompanied by all manner of social disintegration, with marriage break-up, drug-taking and criminal activity all rising rapidly. Faced with such problems many people are so desperate as to hope that religion (which they themselves have long since ceased having anything to do with) might be able to help sort things out, by instilling in the minds of the young and impressionable and unruly 'family' or 'traditional' values. How this is supposed to happen when so few people have anything to do with the Church is unclear, quite apart from it not being at all self-evident what such values actually amount to.

There are very few dogmatically militant atheists, that is people who are certain in their own minds about the non-existence of God, and also vehemently opposed to religion. Most people are simply supremely uninterested in the whole thing, and so can't even qualify as agnostics. It's not a case that they don't feel able to come to a view, and are therefore keeping an open mind pending the arrival of new evidence one way or another. The reality is that they couldn't care less about religion, and simply get on with their lives without giving it a second (or even a first) thought. Most practical atheists are therefore not people who believe that there is no God; rather, they simply do not believe that there *is* a God. Our society is now so secular that the default setting is one of practical atheism; and unless people opt out of this position, and actively adopt a religious worldview, their general outlook will be one where religion plays no part in their everyday lives.

Humanism has roughly the same meaning as atheism, but because it has a rather more positive ring (expressing faith in humanity rather than lack of faith in God) it is the label that many atheists prefer. Religious people often think of atheism as essentially negative, seeing its whole point as the undermining of faith. This is why many Christians regard militant atheists as the enemy, because in addition to holding views that are contrary to those of Christianity, they also have the temerity to express them vigorously. But just as a healthy system of democratic government depends on the existence of a vigorous opposition, a healthy Christianity needs people who subject its claims to the closest possible scrutiny. This should encourage Christians to think more carefully about the sort of things they say, and will also make clear the issues that separate them from many thinking people. It's all too easy for Christians to live in a religious ghetto, going to church, going to Bible study groups, going on Christian holidays, reading avowedly Christian publications, and so on. We *need* people who see Christianity as a silly (and maybe even reprehensible) business to help us sharpen up our arguments, as well as to remind us that the rest of society exists and that there are other well-founded ways of looking at the world.

Much of the attention of atheist writers is directed against the more ridiculous claims that are made in the name of Christianity, and their strictures apply far less to the more subtle ideas of liberal Christianity. Atheism and Christianity are often seen as occupying opposite poles, but the reality is a lot more complex, as is shown by the fact that some people describe their position as one of 'Christian atheism' or 'religious humanism'. Although apparently a contradiction, this is the view that it *is* possible to take Christianity seriously without also subscribing to a variety of metaphysical doctrines, or signing up to a whole series of peculiar ideas.

Atheism has long been used in a pejorative way to denigrate those who dare to think new religious ideas. This included early Christians, such as the 2nd-century Justin Martyr, who embraced the term insofar as it applied to the gods of the pagan world, 'but not with regard to the most true God'. Those Christians who have moved beyond the God of theism may therefore cheerfully plead guilty to the charge of atheism, but would also add 'but not with regard to the most true God'. In other words, it's a dispute as to the adequacy of different ways of conceiving God, rather than a denial that the word 'God' has any useful work to do. When Nietzsche introduced the 19th century to the idea of the 'Death of God', he was highlighting the fact that the very concept of God had gone dead for most people in the West. God can be said to be even more dead today, and the crucial question for Open Christians is whether there is any possibility of breathing new life back into the concept, so that it can resonate with all those people for whom it is stone cold.

The majority of Christians are unlikely to be terribly sympathetic to these ideas, but Open Christians will accept the validity of many of the criticisms made of Christianity by atheism, and explore new, post-theistic ways of working with the God-symbol. Instead of limiting God to the anthropomorphic version so beloved by religious conservatives, we need to expand it to include the non theistic idea of God as the depth and centre of all Being, or the non realist idea of God as the personalized sum of our values – or even take seriously (*and literally*) the orthodox idea that God is Love. Outraged and uncomprehending theists may say that such understandings are atheistic, whereas those who hold such views would say that they most certainly continue to believe in God. The important thing, however, is not the label used (or shouted) but whether the idea helps people who are currently disenfranchised from Christianity to take it seriously.

Chapter 21

THINKING ABOUT POSTMODERNISM

It's hard to avoid postmodernism, and there are lots of good reasons why we shouldn't try to. By its very nature it's difficult to pin down, but it might usefully be linked to the idea of the avant-garde, the essence of which is pioneering. Avant-garde music or theatre is at the opposite pole to what is widely popular; it's usually hard to understand, which is why it's often ridiculed or dismissed. After a while it may become accepted into the mainstream (as happened with Picasso, for example) but then it ceases to be avant-garde. In other words, to say that something is avant-garde is to make a statement about its cultural position rather than about its intrinsic nature. Postmodernism is not so much a school of thought as a rejection of the very *idea* of 'a school of thought': Lyotard talked of 'incredulity towards metanarratives', and this means it is pluriform, multi-faceted and eclectic. It is a revolt against order and system and grand narratives, even seriousness itself. The contrast between Monty Python and most earlier humour brings this out: Python was chaotic, irreverent, untidy; nothing was sacred. Postmodernism is anarchic, ironic, sceptical, experimental, provisional. In computer terms it's a

WYSIWYG worldview, with nothing hidden: don't look for what's 'underneath', because there isn't anything!

The postmodern world is a very different place to the one that went before. It lacks the old certainties, and it also lacks the old optimisms. They were the result of a much more closed culture, together with a view of science as essentially benevolent. Our world is a place of flux, a place where questions are greatly outnumbered by answers: and in the face of the resulting confusion many people cling desperately to nostalgia and fantasy. Many pubs reflect this, with their plastic Tudor beams and fake horse brasses, and much of our religion is the same: wallowing in the past, and offering to transport people back to a world of Certainty (with a capital C). And although there's definitely a market for it (as is shown by the numbers attending those churches which claim to offer it) many people find such an idea an affront to their intellectual integrity, and steer well clear.

The rejection of grand theories and worldviews by postmodernism, however, comes up against the problem of itself: the rejecting of metanarratives is based on the assumption that nothing is beyond questioning, *and that must also include such a view!* The assertion of relativism as if it were in some peculiar way 'True' (with a capital T) is verging on a contradiction. This is not to say that postmodernism isn't worth bothering with, but simply to point out the paradox that is at the heart of its way of seeing things.

Western philosophy began with Plato, and he encouraged people to play down the significance of the way the world *seemed*, and to focus instead on what lay underneath. Metaphysics is the study of the (claimed) hidden dimensions of the world; and because theists think of God as *the* supreme metaphysical reality, any attack on the notion of 'hiddenness' is bound to be seen as an attack on the notion of God. Postmodernism, therefore, has an uneasy, paradoxical relationship with God, and is seen by many people as a threat to religion. It's certainly a threat to the Platonic order, the idea of eternal and changeless reality; and it's therefore also a threat to the security that results from feeling that one knows one's way around the world pretty well. Perhaps the most important postmodern theological question that can be asked is whether God can break free from the chains of metaphysics.

In Nietzsche's story of the Madman, he's rushing about shouting 'I'm looking for God!' He doesn't find him, of course, and his failure to do so tears him apart. God was what gave spiritual light to the earth, and now that, according to Nietzsche, God is Dead (in Nietzsche's words, 'belief in God has become unbelievable') everything is getting steadily darker. The God who has died is the moral God, the God who laid down the rules of behaviour. It is also the metaphysical God, the God of underlying order. In other words, the Death of God is the death also of objective ethics *and* metaphysics. The fixed points have gone, and we realise, for the first time, that we're on our own in the universe: and have to make everything up ourselves.

Nietzsche was all too well aware of what the realisation of this would mean. He appreciated that people would stop up their ears to keep the news away. This is why, over a hundred years after Nietzsche announced the Death of God, the idea is still too new for most people to take on board. In other words, it's still avant-garde, the theological equivalent of Stockhausen, sounding to most people like peculiar noises and not to be taken seriously, and this applies as much to those who go nowhere near churches as to the faithful.

It's difficult enough to get people to take seriously the idea of biblical criticism, but that is as nothing when it comes to trying to introduce the ideas of postmodernism, the essence of which, as Crossan wrote, is that 'there is no lighthouse keeper. There is no lighthouse. There is no dry land. There are only people living on rafts made from their own imaginations. And there is the sea.' A century earlier Nietzsche foresaw this when he wrote 'at last the horizon lies free before us, even granted that it is not bright; at least the sea, our sea, lies open before us. Perhaps there has never been so open a sea'. It is part of the received wisdom of orthodoxy to understand God as being Absolute Truth. But to the postmodernist the very notion of Absolute Truth is meaningless. Objective Truth has gone, and the Objective God has gone with it, which is hardly surprising if they are one and the same.

Most people, of course, whether sympathetic, hostile or simply indifferent to religion, all play the same Objective Truth game: religious propositions (like all propositions) must be either true or not true, even if there is no consensus about the criteria for establishing which they are. Religious postmodernists (who are usually also non realists) refuse to classify things in this way and thus provoke fury in both theists and atheists, together with bafflement in almost everyone else. Religious people see them as closet atheists who don't believe in God but persist in playing at religion; whilst atheists see them as fellow non-believers, but who lack the courage to admit to themselves that religion is nonsense. The reason for the venom of many of the attacks is that the non realist is postulating a situation very unlike that of modernism or before, whose world was knowable, fairly user-friendly and, above all, structured. There was 'truth out there' and the more of it we could get into our heads the better off we'd be.

The new model is of a disturbing flux, a void, a transience. There is no grounding in an eternal, quasi-Platonic order; there is nothing on which a dogmatic edifice can be built. In the conventional model Truth equals Power, but with postmodernism, because Truth (with a capital T) has no place, there is no hierarchy of power, and hence no attempt made to force others into its mould. It is thus not so much a belief, as *freedom from belief*; it is necessarily pluralist and is playfully ironic, realising the essential paradox that lies at the heart of any relativistic position.

It sees religion as providing a set of symbols and a store of stories, with the Church operating as a sort of theatrical costumier in which people can feel free to rummage and make of the material what they will. Such freedom is unsettling to those who need to have fixed boundaries, but for those who are freer spirits it provides an opportunity for a more adequate sense of the numinous to emerge. An analogy may help: orthodox Christianity is like classical music, with a fixed score; liberal Christianity is like traditional jazz, with a core melody, but some scope for improvisation; postmodern Christianity is like avant-garde jazz, with almost unlimited opportunities to explore themes in your own way.

The only really safe option is the first: if the musicians play *exactly* what is written in the score in front of them it means that members of the audience, if they want, can follow the piece, note by note, in the same way that people can follow Bible readings in church. But jazz won't allow that: if the musicians stick to a score, by definition they're not playing jazz! Breaking free from the score is a risky, uncomfortable and unpredictable thing: once a piece is underway neither the audience nor the musicians know precisely what's going to happen or where the piece is going to go. There's a tension about the performance, the musical equivalent of a leap of faith.

Jazz is a deeply subversive art form, but this is hardly surprising given the social and political conditions in which it originated. Avant-garde jazz pushes the boundaries as far as they will go (and well beyond what most people can cope with) which is why it is such a good way of picturing radical faith. Bertrand Russell said that it required considerable courage to set out into the unknown in this way, but added 'in the end the fresh air brings vigour, and the great spaces have a splendour of their own'. As an avowed atheist, that was the sort of thing he would be expected to say, of course. But just as the devil need not always have the best tunes, there's no reason why religious jazz shouldn't be as exciting as any other kind.

Chapter 22

THINKING ABOUT SEX

Sex is not a subject much discussed in Christian circles in anything other than a negative sense. It tends to raise its head only in connection with 'problems', such as 'the problem of homosexuality' (especially homosexual clergy). Many Christians (but not only Christians) see sex as something rather embarrassing, not very nice really, and therefore to be talked or thought about or indeed engaged in as little as possible. (I would like to think this is something of an exaggeration, but fear that it isn't). The result is that Christianity, yet again, thoroughly deserves its reputation for being opposed to many of the most enjoyable aspects of life, an attitude which adds to the plethora of other reasons that people have for steering well clear of it.

Such a situation is very unfortunate, because things don't have to be like this, despite the fact that for many centuries there has been a desperately negative approach to what are rather quaintly called 'the pleasures of the flesh'. It's easy to find lots of biblical texts (especially from St Paul) to justify this attitude, and it sometimes seems that those with an unhealthy amount of self-hatred seize these on with relief. Society in general has a very ambivalent attitude towards sex: on the one hand we are awash with sexual images, whilst on the other hand the idea of a woman breast-feeding in public is widely frowned-on.

There's a distinct lack of joined-up thinking, partly as a result of many people failing to understand the strength and diversity of human sexual desire.

This is exemplified in a religion that celebrates babies but tries not to think too much about how they come into being. Christianity should help people to enjoy life to the full, within the bounds of propriety – but this is where the problems start! Those bounds are not fixed, and what is unacceptable at one time may become acceptable (at least to a much larger number of people) at another. Some will have a black-and-white approach, and say that certain ways of behaving are always wrong, on the grounds that they can point to verses in the Bible that prohibit them. Others may be completely unpersuaded by such arguments, either because they have no interest in what the Bible says, or, in the case of liberal Christians, because they do not think that present-day behaviour can be so easily deduced.

Debate about sexual behaviour tends to divide along the lines of those who see morals as flexible servants, and those who see them as inflexible masters. Those in the former group are likely to be fairly relaxed about the sorts of things they find acceptable, whereas those in the latter tend to be a lot more certain, and therefore probably a lot fiercer in their judgements, about such matters as homosexuality. Evangelicals see this as either a disease or a sin, whilst liberals tend to see it as part of the infinite variety of things, and as such morally neutral. The unease that many Christians have about sex is particularly marked with regard to the sexuality of the clergy (with Evangelicals in particular finding the very idea of homosexual clergy so offensive as to be unacceptable). In broader terms there may be considerable unease at the idea that many of the clergy have very active sex lives; the old idea still lingers that taking the spiritual life seriously is incompatible with taking sex seriously as well.

Human sexuality is a richly complex thing, and varies both in nature and intensity. Some people seem able to live a sex-free existence with equanimity, whilst others find sex a vital part of everyday life. Given the biological order of things it would be surprising if this *wasn't* the case, but given the age-profile of most Anglican congregations it is also hardly surprising that many churchgoers find the subject of little personal relevance. This does point to the very real danger that the Church can easily seem out of touch when we pay so little attention, in any positive way, to a subject that occupies such a large proportion of the waking thoughts of so many people in our society.

Sex is such a central (and natural) part of human life that there is something bizarre about people complaining when it is shown in films or on television. It is also very curious that media portrayal of violence between two people is seen as a far more acceptable subject than sex between two people. Christianity is often correctly seen as being joyless and life-denying, and the way that enormous esteem is shown to members of religious orders who have renounced most of the things that are ordinarily considered to give pleasure (especially sex) seems to indicate the degree to which many people are deeply suspicious about the flesh, and admire those who 'have overcome' it. But perhaps such 'thanatophiliacs' (people with an unhealthy interest in death) should be more pitied than admired? What is so wonderful about giving up pleasures? It might be considered outrageous to suggest that anyone who voluntarily turns their back on things that give joy may be suffering from some form of personality disorder, but it does need to be said, loudly and clearly, that Christianity does not have to be opposed to sensuality, even though many of its practitioners may be.

In response to the question 'is sex dirty?' Woody Allen replied 'only if it's done right', and the point is well made. There is absolutely no reason why vigorous, full-blown, passionate, decidedly carnal sex shouldn't be celebrated, at least as much as the gentler, more decorous version that is perhaps more widespread (and is certainly more respectable). Of course sex isn't all that there is to relationships; of course affection and love and respect are vital. But sex is not an insignificant part either, and the very fact that even to say this sort of thing may be deemed shocking is itself a sad state of affairs.

Why did sex get such a bad name? How did it ever get thought of as something to be ashamed about, rather than something to be enjoyed? Early Christian teaching, based on certain passages in the Bible, has to bear much of the responsibility, with its emphasis on the need to mortify the flesh so that the soul might take wings. Christianity grew in soil provided by Greek philosophy, and the result was a religion that unfortunately had many life-denying characteristics. It is high time that this ended, because there was never any good reason for it in the first place! We need to celebrate the erotic, to glory in the physical, because they are aspects of life that bring pleasure. Engaging in sexual activity solely for pleasure is traditionally deemed to be 'lustful', and has long been widely condemned by the Church. But although the main biological reason for sex is obviously reproduction, there is no reason why that should be seen as the only (or indeed the main) reason for engaging in it. Sex may also be seen as promoting bonding, and could also improve health: but mainly it is very pleasurable – and the more pleasure there is in the world, the better.

In the 16th century, the spread of syphilis throughout Europe was seen by the Church as God's punishment for lust, and it opposed attempts at both prevention and treatment. The appalling amount of suffering which resulted has been replicated to some extent in the contemporary spread of AIDS, which has also been seen by many conservative Christians as God's punishment for promiscuity, and especially homosexual promiscuity. It is no coincidence that there is considerable overlap between (i) those whose doorway to the sacred is the God of theism, (ii) those who believe that such a God inflicts punishment on people, (iii) those who see things in very clear and definite terms, and (iv) those who are particularly condemnatory about sexual behaviour. These are people for whom the concepts of wrath, judgement and punishment are key parts of their religious worldview; regrettably they also tend to be people who are keen that their views are imposed on others.

The prudish obsession with sex means that it dominates the field of morality to such an extent that many more destructive aspects of human behaviour are given a pretty easy ride. Within congregations people can be cruel, greedy, sarcastic, proud, critical, judgemental, hypocritical, backbiting, gossipy – and get away with it. But the slightest whiff of sexual indiscretion, and there's hell to pay! Of course, sexual behaviour can be exploitative, of course it can be manipulative, of course it can be thoroughly degrading. But so can all sorts of other behaviour as well. There is nothing inherent in sexual behaviour that means it is especially likely to have such undesirable features. If we take Christianity seriously we are bound to see that love needs to inform everything that we do. To love others means (among other things) to respect them, to treat them as ends and not means: in short, to take their needs seriously. If our sexual behaviour is grounded upon such love, then there is every possibility that it will enhance rather than diminish all concerned. As Augustine put it: 'love – and do what you like'.

Chapter 23

THINKING ABOUT
NEW AGE RELIGION

Recent years have seen lots more people involved in religious fringe groups, cults and sects. Whilst the mainstream churches have been declining (apart from the growth in the Fundamentalist and Evangelical wings) many people have been attracted to the enormous number of new religious groups and movements. Some of these are termed 'New Age' and incorporate a wide variety of ideas and activities, many of which grew out of the hippie counter-culture of the 1960s. They include such things as support for/belief in paganism, witchcraft, UFOs, astral projection, Tarot cards, crystals, feng shui, vegetarianism, communal living, renewable energy, alternative medicine, the Green movement, ouija boards, astrology, deep ecology, the channelling of spirits, reincarnation, and so on.

This is such a disparate group that it simply isn't possible to have an overall view about its members: to say that you're 'in favour' of them, is as unintelligent as 'being opposed' to them. Some may seem ludicrous or dangerous, others entirely benign, but each needs to be considered on its merits. Those activities that involve the occult attract particular hostility, especially from conservative Christians who see any way of thinking about the world that is not solidly Bible-based as highly suspect. But such a clearly focused approach is completely alien to the philosophy of New Age, whose essence is its chaotic diversity.

This is itself a reflection and expression of postmodernism (see Chapter 21), and reflects the breaking down of unitary ways of seeing reality in general, and religion in particular. Increasing numbers of people have cast aside the restrictions of traditional religion, and set out on their own particular faith paths, some of which are very peculiar. The essential thing about the New Age phenomenon is that it is syncretist and eclectic, which its critics term the 'pick-and-mix' approach. This offers a very significant challenge to the way we approach religion. It urges us to be a lot bolder, willing (and indeed eager) to explore other faith traditions, and combine their teachings in a way that works best for us. It acts as a protest against the perceived narrowness of sticking to a single path. The fluidity of ideas in New Age thinking is predicated on a basis of tolerant pluralism, whereas conventional religious thinking all too often regards ideas that are different as being rivals, which therefore need to be overcome and silenced. Much New Age material looks like (and is!) gobbledegook, but its critics (and maybe its liberal friends) might say the same about some of the writings of Christianity.

Once we recognise the multi-faceted nature of reality, we will *expect* people to explore this in all sorts of different ways, some of which we will not understand or sympathise with. Conservative Christians see accordance with orthodoxy as the yardstick by which ideas should be judged. Liberal/Open Christians adopt more pragmatic criteria, namely whether the ideas in question lead people to grow. If they tend to help those who follow them become more loving and kind, then they are probably worth bothering with. If, on the other hand, they make them more narrow and rigid and judgemental, then probably we'd be better off without them.

The problem is that being open to all sorts of ideas from all sorts of places can easily lead to such an uncritical approach that anything is welcomed, no matter how wacky. Open Christians may be critical of orthodox religious ideas but naively enthusiastic about silly and even bizarre New Age concepts. Inconsistency is never to be recommended, and if one religious path is to be judged in terms of its intellectual rigor, the same touchstone *must* be applied to the other. Although the postmodern world (see Chapter 21) is a much more open place, and although barminess may to an extent be in the eye of the beholder, there must still be *some* criteria to distinguish the reasonable from the ludicrous. There's something laughable about the way that many people in the West have dismissed Christianity as being self-evidently absurd, but gone on to embrace New Age or Eastern religion, which any disinterested observer might find even more so!

New Age thinking is holistic, which means that its ideas penetrate every aspect of life. Although Christianity is supposed to be like this, in practice it often functions as a sort of bolt-on, with the rest of life going on much as before. It's this all-embracing quality which means that New Age *thinking* can also be thought of as New Age *religion*. But it's a very different sort of religion to Christianity, with no organisation, no leaders and no creed. And this unmanageable and unpredictable diversity can seem threatening to those who have a rigid view of what can count as truth, and who therefore can't cope with the chaotic openness of the New Age approach.

At the heart of this holistic thinking is the earth. New Agers revere the planet and its web of life, seeing it not simply as a resource to be exploited but a gift to be treasured. From this starting point it follows that we need to be more frugal in our use of energy and raw materials and learn to live with far fewer possessions. The health of the environment is seen as far more important than the health of the economy, and this is summed-up in two of the most famous New Age phrases: 'Think globally – act locally', and 'Small is Beautiful'. Such an approach can be applied not just in economic terms, but also in religious terms. This means that the religious outlook of the New Age is very much one of decentralisation, with truth being discovered from the bottom upwards, rather than given, magisterium-fashion, from the top downwards.

The emphasis on the small and the local and the home-grown is reflected in the way that New Age spirituality respects all religious traditions, and sees all sorts of roads leading to God (truth), with spiritual growth occurring as a result of people choosing their own path rather than following the dogmas that are other people's paths. Rather than stressing our sinfulness, it focuses on our potential, and on the joy that can be found if we live fully and indeed exuberantly in the present. Truth is to be found in the search itself, and the emphasis is on openness and journeying, rather than on closure and arriving.

The disparate, even chaotic nature of New Age thinking provides a far better model for the religious approach to life than the highly structured, hierarchical, dogmatic and intolerant version so favoured by religious conservatives. This is because the New Age approach recognises that the world is such a wonderfully complex and mysterious place that we need all the insights we can get, from wherever we can get them. To limit ourselves to those from one single tradition is to be wilfully and culpably ignorant, and Open Christians are almost bound to share the pluralist and anti-dogmatic stance of the New Age movement. They will be keen to explore all sorts of traditions and combine elements from them into a unique personal synthesis that, like the New Age movement, takes seriously the need to respect the integrity of the Earth and the web of life that it supports.

Chapter 24

THINKING ABOUT
THE SUPERNATURAL

'Supernatural' – the word itself conjures up all sorts of images, many of them rather creepy. If someone is said to be interested in the supernatural it suggests they watch horror films, visit mediums, go on ghost hunts, and similar odd things. But many Christians have an interest in it. In fact, some might say that this is a prerequisite of *being* a Christian. But what *is* 'the supernatural', and how might it relate to an understanding of Christianity that is appropriate for the 21st century?

It is sometimes said that science deals with 'the natural' world, and religion with 'the supernatural', that reality which is claimed to lie 'beyond' the natural world and therefore 'outside' the realm of science. Heaven and hell (see Chapter 33) together with God, have been traditionally 'located' in the supernatural realm, which by definition is not open to scientific investigation. Miracles (see Chapter 12) might be thought of as occasions when the supernatural 'breaks into' the ordinary world, and which by definition cannot be scientifically understood.

But what does such a claim amount to? What is there in the world that *cannot* be dealt with by science? Is it being suggested that there are aspects of reality that can never (even in principle) be understood rationally, or measured by scientific equipment? If so, how might such things be identified in the first place? The supernatural and the paranormal seem to have a particular appeal to the psychologically disturbed and emotionally fragile, together with those who have a mistrust of science and a distrust of thinking. That there are significant numbers of such people, clinging to a magical, enchanted view of the world, shows that the Enlightenment has still, for many, only got a toe-hold in the 21st century. They have little or no interest in trying to *understand* the world, because to say that something 'has a supernatural explanation' is not to explain it at all, but to say that we can *never* know its cause. It might even be a way of saying that we don't think it had a cause at all, although such a claim makes no sense and is simply a collection of words strung together to make what appears to be a meaningful proposition. To say 'God caused it' is equally unhelpful, because it is simply another way of expressing the view that we don't know (and can never know) what caused it.

It is very possible that there exist all sorts of objects and forces in the universe of which we currently have no knowledge but which we might do one day. Scientists may, eventually, be able to account for phenomena such as ESP, which at present is a mystery. But if they did, it wouldn't prove that paranormal phenomena exist; rather it would show that our view of the way human beings communicate with one another had been too limited, and needed to be enlarged.

The whole area of the paranormal and the supernatural is particularly favoured by those who can't, or won't, engage in careful thinking, and who are both gullible and scientifically illiterate. The word 'science' itself is sometimes used as a bit of a frightener, with many religious people being keen to point out ways in which science (strictly speaking, technology) can be misused, or areas in which it is unable to give all the answers: only the dim-witted would expect that it *could* do this, but there are plenty of them about, and they often seem to have the loudest voices!

There is no need for religion to see science as a rival: each is trying to do a different job, just as poetry does not compete with physics in trying to describe the world. Religion, alongside poetry and music and physics and all the rest, is part of the range of ways in which human beings respond to the wonder of being alive. The world can be looked at from so many different perspectives that it is absurd to try and privilege one above the other. It's a question of 'appropriateness': some situations require one approach, others require another. One size can *never* fit all, and to insist, in the name of 'orthodoxy' that it can, is a sign of lazy-mindedness, dogmatism and desperation.

The decline in belief in the supernatural among many intelligent people has been paralleled by a growth in it within congregations that have been part of the charismatic renewal movement, where all sorts of strange things occur: 'faith healing', 'exorcism', 'speaking in tongues', together with uncontrollable laughing, screaming, barking, crying, falling over and so on. This revival of what is really a medieval way of looking at the world is both grotesque and dangerous, especially in view of its undoubted appeal to the disturbed and vulnerable, and the way in which such developments serve to alienate still further those people who are generally sympathetic to Christianity, but who couldn't for one moment contemplate becoming involved with such practices.

Our whole way of relating to the world is premised on thinking and reasoning: if my car doesn't start, I expect the garage mechanic to investigate it and then solve the problem. If he said that he couldn't, because its failure to work is due to supernatural agencies (which is a particular way of saying that its failure to work has no cause) I would conclude not that he was gifted with peculiar insight, but that he was either joking, or incompetent – or mad. But from the charismatic perspective, people who are suffering from mental illness and are what would normally be called mad, may be said to be 'possessed by the devil', and needing the attentions, not of a psychiatrist but of an exorcist. It is very much the world of the Middle Ages, but without the excuse that people of those times had.

Many of the churches that focus on the supernatural have experienced rapid growth in numbers, which shows that they are providing what people *want* – which of course may be far from what they *need*. Society is currently facing the enormous problems of drug addiction, with very large numbers of people engaged in behaviour that is addictive, irrational and antisocial. Their lives are often so focused on their habit that they may consciously shun contact with families and friends. If religion leads people to behave in similarly peculiar, irrational ways, if it has the effect that they isolate themselves from non-Christians and centre themselves on their own chosen group, then it's clearly a worrying phenomenon. And far from seeking to try and emulate them, the rest of the Church needs to try and reduce the amount of psychological damage that may result from such activities.

Within many churches there is an extraordinary amount of un-reason, with science being seen as an enemy instead of being regarded as a magnificent testimony to human intelligence and endeavour. There is nothing constraining about scientific 'laws'; these are descriptive not prescriptive, and therefore can never be 'broken': if they do not work in all observable situations, (as is supposedly the case with miracles) it shows that they are inadequate and need to be revised. To discount reason, or to turn one's back on reason, is to open the way for all sorts of political and religious ideological nonsense.

Supernaturalism does exactly this, by setting out its stall in the garden of superstition. Anything that is 'supernatural' is, by definition, inaccessible to reason, and so tales of miraculous healings, even raisings from the dead, abound, unchallenged (and unchallengeable) by being required to produce objective and independently verified evidence. It is a world of 'signs and wonders', a world of the febrile imagination, a world which a supernatural deity periodically invades in response to prayer (see Chapter 4).

Open Christianity welcomes a variety of perspectives, but that of supernaturalism can lead to problems if given too free a rein. The test is, does the particular religious standpoint result in people becoming more open and loving and affirming, or does it lead to them becoming more inward-looking, dogmatic and judgemental? Is it based on intolerance and ignorance? Does it see other perspectives (including non-religious ones) as threatening or enriching? Does it see religion as a means or as an end? One of the dangers of supernaturalism is that it plays down the importance of *this* world and *this* life, with the result that social, political and environmental problems may get less attention than they merit.

Superstitions may be thought of as the remnants of old religious beliefs; the reason they appear bizarre and disconnected is because the thought-world to which they originally belonged has faded away. Those who visit holy shrines in the hope of miraculous cures are involved in superstition because although people in the Middle Ages thought that such things were possible, it is not how we think today. The secularisation of Western societies means that increasingly the *whole* of Christianity looks like this, and the greater the emphasis on supernaturalism, the fewer people will want anything to do with any of it. It needs to be made clear that more and more Christians are *also* unable to make any sense of a supernatural realm, and look with horror at the way in which all sorts of primitive superstitiousness is making a return into relatively mainstream churches.

The good news for the intelligent outsiders is that they need not feel obliged to try and understand in a literal way ideas that have enormous power when taken symbolically and metaphorically. Significant numbers of churchgoers are finding a sense of freedom and excitement as they leave the supernatural aspects of faith behind. This does not apply to all (or even the majority) of church members, but there are enough who think in this way to show that non-supernatural approaches to religion really *are* capable of supporting people's weight, and providing the spiritual nourishment they need.

Chapter 25

THINKING ABOUT SILENCE

The world is such a complex place that we can easily feel out of our depth. There is simply so much to know, so much to try and understand, that there is a very real danger of being overwhelmed by it all. Fortunately, help is always to hand in the form of the tabloids and the many pedlars of simplistic nostrums. Their dedicated labours mean that no one ever need feel baffled or overawed, because they make it possible for anyone to understand anything, even very difficult ideas. No matter what the issue, it can be summed up in a few sentences, and people guided to a genuine understanding. *At least that's the widely held picture.*

The truth is, of course, very different, in that the worldview people acquire as a result of all this is so crude that there is little resemblance between it and reality. It simply is not possible to turn the world into a straightforward place; any simple picture is bound to be inadequate, perhaps even a travesty. This is as true in politics as it is in science, but the democratic system leads people to think that not only does their view count (via the ballot box) as much as anyone else's, but so does their opinion. This latter is plainly false, in that some people's views are well considered and well informed, whilst others are neither. It is obvious that in scientific matters the opinions of scientists carry far more weight than those of non-scientists, not least because it may only be scientists who actually understand the issues. To be well informed means taking time and trouble, combining intelligence with thought; and this is true of *any* field of human endeavour. People whose knowledge of political affairs is limited to what they see in bold headlines on the front of the tabloids are bound to have less grasp of the complexities and subtleties involved than those who spend a lot more time and effort wrestling with the issues.

The problem is that the limited (and supposedly declining) attention spans of most people mean that there is a widespread expectation of instant familiarity, with anything and everything. No matter what the issue or subject, there is an implicit assumption that neither time nor trouble (nor indeed intelligence) are essential prerequisites for an adequate understanding. It's the same with theology (see Chapter 17): very few people have much of an interest in it, but considerable numbers feel more than qualified to offer views on it, no matter how flimsily based these may be. As a general rule, the more forcefully and dogmatically someone's views are expressed, the less understanding tends to lie behind them.

Behind all this is the general unwillingness of most people to admit, either to themselves or to anyone else, how ignorant they actually are. The word 'ignorance' comes from a Latin root meaning 'not to know'. And although there is no shame in this, most people seem unable to say that they don't know something. But acknowledged ignorance is the only honest response to most of life: partly because there's so *much* to know and so little time and energy at our disposal; and partly because there are so many things that are simply way beyond our capacity (and in some cases beyond *anyone's* capacity) ever to know. Hiding our ignorance means that we end up with a very distorted view of the world, one that is far less wonderful and awesome than the reality deserves. Not knowing is one thing, but hiding from the fact that we don't know is a way of shielding our eyes from truth: which, in religious terms, is a way of hiding from God.

Plato took the search for truth with absolute seriousness, but was very scathing about democracy. In similar fashion we need to have the courage to separate the search for truth from shows of hands, and if necessary brave the charge of elitism. Popular and populist as it is, conservative religion is characterised by its overweening sense of confidence, the result of a very narrow view of the world. The more conscious you are of your ignorance, the less strident you are likely to be in your utterances, whilst the narrower your view, the less likely you are to be aware of the extent and depth of your ignorance.

Ignorance lies at the very heart of religion. When this is *conscious ignorance*, the result is a quiet, thoughtful openness; but when it is *unconscious ignorance*, the result is usually mindless, often scary, invariably depressing. Silence is probably the most appropriate (and certainly the most profound) religious response: it makes no claims, and deceives no one. But like any spiritual discipline it can be hard work: and very troubling. It throws us back on ourselves, with all that that involves. If we are genuinely open and honest about our ignorance, we are forced into silence; and in the silence may find religious truths currently inaudible due to all the noise that we are making. An awareness of our ignorance should make us humble, and draw us into the silence that is the contemplation of truth.

Silence has long been an important part of religion and could usefully be practised a lot more widely. Prayer (see Chapter 4) is usually a desperately wordy affair, but true silence demands a cessation of words, both spoken and thought. Silence leading to emptiness is an aspect of the spiritual life which has such potential to help us grow that perhaps we need to be more up-front when we come across the unconscious ignorance that announces itself in the form of great sweeping religious statements, invariably proclaimed with unyielding confidence. Until and unless people are brought face-to-face with their religious ignorance, until and unless they are reduced to silence in the face of the glorious grandeur and tragedy and Mystery of life, there is little hope of God ever getting a look-in.

The words we use are often intended to help us get a purchase on the world, so that we feel at home there. Until the rise of Romanticism in the 18th century, people did not enjoy or appreciate the wild and rugged scenery of mountains, with places like the Lake District (and still more the Alps) being thought of as 'barren and frightful'. Once it became the fashion to visit them, however, their beauty and grandeur became highly prized and greatly enjoyed, but it needed a major cultural shift before this was possible. Part of this negative view of Nature may have been due to the fact that the world at that time was still a threatening, mysterious place that was largely untamed. Until people learned how to control and domesticate it, they couldn't relax in it. But once they had acquired control over it, its power to frighten disappeared.

Religion explores a world that is far more mysterious and untamed than 18th-century mountain wildernesses, and so it's hardly surprising that most people, if they venture into the territory at all, feel the need to take with them survival kits containing lots of words as a way of helping them to feel at home there. After all, if we can *say* lots of things about Ultimate Mystery, then presumably it must show that we really *do* know our way around?

Wishful thinking, of course, but perfectly understandable. Those who are the least secure in their faith tend to be the ones who say the most (and indeed, tend to say it loudest and most dogmatically – in the same sort of way that someone might whistle in the dark, to reassure themselves that everything is all right). But it's now time for those who are perhaps more courageous travellers and explorers, to stand up and be counted. They need to make it clear that although the spiritual landscape is very much unknown territory, they are prepared to venture into it without all the baggage that earlier travellers felt was necessary. The first climbers who went up Everest without oxygen were thought to be foolhardy, but they showed that it really was possible to exist up there without it.

The Zen tradition stresses the importance to the spiritual life of faith, doubt and courage: doubt as a way of keeping alive the mystery and the perplexity at the heart of life; faith as the willingness to stay with that mystery; and courage as the strength needed to avoid taking easy ways out and adopting off the peg 'answers'. It is an approach that openly acknowledges that with regard to the profound questions of life we simply do not know what is going on, which is why words tend to get in the way.

Religion has been described as 'Silence qualified by Parables', and in similar vein it might be said that the only adequate response to Mystery is Silence qualified by Art. At present, much of the running in religion is being made by the voices of mind-numbingly confident banality. They are bound to continue to make the most noise, for the same sort of reasons that the number of people listening to Radio 1 is always going to exceed the number who listen to Radio 3. But there are other strands to religion, and they need to be recognised and welcomed. The sooner more thoughtful and intelligent (and silent!) voices are heard, giving the space for reflection and contemplation and sheer Be-ing that is provided by holy silence, the sooner religion will become less embarrassing and more available to those who find what's currently on offer about as unattractive as it could be. And the sooner *that* happens, the better.

that they went straight into the Church at birth, having come from clergy families, and having breathed the rarefied air of ecclesiastica forever. This is all rather off-putting for those on the outside. The Church begins to take on the air of a closed club, and the less fashionable it becomes to go to church, the more this is the case.

Evangelism is about breaking out of this straitjacket, and finding ways of taking the message (that we claim is worth bothering with) to people who have little time for it at the moment. But much of what is normally thought of as evangelism is crude and cringeworthy. Essentially it consists of shouting the same sort of things louder and more often; and although this may be what some people want (and perhaps even need) it is not going to make an impact on most thoughtful people. And it is thoughtful people that particularly need reaching: not because the rest aren't worth bothering with, but because their needs tend to be catered for by the evangelism that is already going on.

Most people inside the Church have little or no idea of the chasm that separates them from the rest of society, and this in itself is probably the biggest single obstacle to evangelism. The main reason why the great majority of people would sooner do almost anything than attend church is that they can't see any point whatsoever in coming. It may well be that the churches have simply got to get used to the idea that what they are offering is not (and never will be) in demand, and plan for terminal decline. It's not about having jollier hymns or more smiley vicars or shorter services, but something far deeper than that. The problem is that the whole idea of the supernatural (see Chapter 24) is simply incredible to many educated people today. Of course, there will always be those who crave such things (as is shown by the numbers involved in wacky religious movements, or the popularity of horror films) but in terms of the intelligent mainstream, the churches have pretty much lost the plot.

The world we live in has, in general, lost its sense of the sacred, its sense of God – and urgently needs to find it again. How this may be brought about is not at all clear; but it certainly *won't* happen by simply repeating the word 'God' over and over again in the way that church people often seem to. We need to find new ways of approaching what is holy, what is sacred, what is ultimate; new ways of approaching the awe and the mystery and the wonder and the glory that the word 'God' has pointed towards. Those things are still around, and human beings still have the same spiritual needs and faculties as they have always had. It is the job of the Church (or at least of those members of the Church who take evangelism seriously *and* who are aware of the impossibility of trying to carry on the business of evangelism as if nothing had changed) to take its courage and its faith in both hands, and dare to launch out into what are, effectively, uncharted waters.

Religion grew up in part as a response to the terror that primitive peoples felt. The world was a frightening place, and disaster could strike at any moment. Something of this still remains, but religion is also the result (and the expression) of wonder and joy, of what has been termed 'Cosmic Gratitude'. A Christianity focused on this can be thought of as *the attempt, using the writings and liturgy of the Church, to express the inexpressible, wrestle with the inexplicable, and learn to live with the incomprehensible.* To put things like this may strike many traditional Christians as such a watered-down faith as to be effectively unrecognisable. But if this actually *is* what lies at the very heart of Christianity, it means that provided someone can subscribe to such a programme, then they can, with a clear conscience, call themselves a Christian.

A Christianity that does not take note of the world we live in, is one that deserves to die. That world has moved on a long way in the last century – let alone the previous 20 centuries! Our society has little time for Christianity as it currently exists. But evangelism tends to be practised most enthusiastically by those who claim that only by following the tenets of their *brand* of their particular *religion* can one 'be saved' – and that seems to require time-travelling back across the centuries, even millennia, to a world when people thought very differently about almost everything.

157

Much of it is gross, offensive stuff, based on a mixture of ignorance and smugness, and reflecting a black-and-white worldview, which divides humanity into the saved and the lost, the blessed and the damned. The 'Decade of Evangelism' showed that there are still plenty of people around who think that unless others come to see things in the same sort of way that they themselves do, their lives will be impoverished. At present, most of the Christians involved in evangelism seem to see contact with others as essentially a one-way transaction – we give, they receive. Until we accept that we *don't* possess truth in its entirety, we will never be open to learning from other religions and traditions.

For the Open Christian, Christ is our doorway to God, to that world of the spirit and the sacred that is unlimited. For members of other faiths there are different doorways, and it doesn't matter through which door people enter: all that's important is that they get inside and are able to experience and explore the Mystery at the heart of everything. It follows that our evangelism must aim at spreading, not Christianity, but a yearning for a pathway into the Sacred. We must try to help people become aware of their spiritual potential, something that can be tapped through art and music as well as through religion.

There are many routes to the Profound, and Christianity is only one strand of one route (that of religion). Each of the world's great religious traditions may be seen as a well, which reaches down to the precious life-giving water at its base. What matters is being able to access this water, being able to drink it, being able to penetrate the depths of what it is to be fully human. Not so much 'Christ the Son of God' as 'Christ the doorway to God – for us'. The groundwater reached by the wells is the religious dimension to life that we usually call 'God'. Christ is one pathway to the Holy, one well – and our evangelism must abandon all attempts to persuade people to move from one well to another.

Chapter 27

THINKING ABOUT IDOLS

From Greenland's icy mountains, one of the most famous of all the Victorian hymns, is hardly ever sung now on the grounds that some of its words are just too offensive. Its second verse concludes *In vain with lavish kindness the gifts of God are strown/the heathen in his blindness bows down to wood and stone*, and is a good example of the dismissive and patronising attitude held by many Victorian Christians towards those of other faiths. The word 'heathen' was used originally of those who lived 'on the heath', in other words, out in the wilds; and the term was then applied to anyone thought to be 'primitive'. Such people were regarded as savages, possessing no insights worth having, and in severe need of conversion. It's never terribly helpful to assume that we are bright and right and others are stupid and wrong: it's arrogant and results in blindness to other ways of looking at things. A much better approach, when faced with behaviour or beliefs that we don't understand, is to look, listen and learn: what at first sight seems ridiculous, may come to make sense.

No one, in their own mind, worships idols: the term is *always* pejorative, and can only be used of those we don't respect. An idol is something that people are devoted to, or focused on, that *in our view* does not seem worthy of such veneration. It is, in other words, *(from our perspective)* a 'false god' – a god that isn't really (or shouldn't be thought of as) a god. This is a totally subjective claim, of course, and can only be made from a particular perspective – in our case, that of Christianity. The Judaeo-Christian tradition has never tried to give physical representation to God, and has therefore found it particularly shocking when other religions do, but it's our problem, not theirs. When people's worship involves the use of carved figures, the safest (and politest) thing to do, instead of assuming that they are simply ignorant, is to say that we simply don't know what's going on, and refrain from leaping to any conclusions until we *do* know.

Our world is also full of secular idols – and once again religious people are terribly good at spotting when other people are taken in by them! Such unworthy objects of devotion are all around: someone's attachment to his car, another's attachment to his social position, another's to his bank balance. We may look at such things and turn our religious noses up, seeing them as unworthy because we think that none of them is capable of satisfying people at the very deepest level. It may be self-evident to us that a person's life *shouldn't* be focused on his football team or his job – but what if he says that he finds it completely satisfying, and maintains that view until his dying day? Do we conclude that he was right and we were wrong? Or do we say that he must have been a poor, sad case, and if he'd had anything about him then he would have come to the conclusion we did? Our incomprehension may be the result of a lack of imagination, or it might be spot on: not knowing which is an example of why many find the postmodern flux (see Chapter 21) so troubling!

But perhaps even more troubling is the realisation that in addition to the secular world being replete with idols, large numbers of Christians are themselves guilty of idolatry. Not only in the sense that many are over-attached to worldly things, but in the sense that enormous numbers cling to religious ideas which are extremely unworthy, and as much idols as the Golden Calf. Freud claimed that God was simply a human projection, and there seems little doubt that the anthropomorphic God is the one that most Christians worship. In

1963, just before the publication of *Honest to God, The Observer* carried an article by Bishop John Robinson, under the famous title 'Our image of God must go'. The article and the book caused an outcry, as well as attracting a great deal of support; but in the long term it all seems to have been to remarkably little avail. The image of God that Robinson was attacking is alive and well, and still stands in need of the sort of revision he was urging 40 years ago.

Eleven years before *Honest to God* J B Phillips had published a little book whose title, *'Your God is too Small'*, sums up the problem of religious idolatry rather nicely. Far too often, the God of the Church is like that. Too small, in that many of those outside the Church, when they look at the God that the Church seems to proclaim, are unable to see anything that can help them in their lives, or indeed anything that they can begin to relate to. Too small, also, in that many of those inside the Church are stuck with an idea which fails to do justice to the mystery and the sheer awesomeness of reality. A God who is far too small, in far too many ways, for far too many people becomes the religious equivalent of the crude and simplistic view of the world served up by the tabloids (see Chapter 25).

The problem, however, is that a bigger God, a more adequate God, a better God-*concept*, one that stands a greater chance of 'working' in the lives of those who are currently God-*less* (without God), is bound to be a riskier God. Religious doctrines and creeds (see Chapter 5) are useful summaries of the way that previous generations have thought about God, but they can all too easily harden into idols. Molten gold, all the while it is in contact with a source of energy, can take on any shape at all; but once it is removed from the heat, and poured into a mould, it begins to harden and assumes a particular form. The gold of the Golden Calf was once free-flowing, and could respond to its environment, but once it was constrained by the mould, it became solid and inflexible. It's the same with doctrines. They grow in response to the needs of their time, but as the centuries pass and circumstances and ideas change, they become detached from the energy that gave birth to them, and end up as hard and inflexible, incapable of responding to the new conditions.

However, once we start to re-envisage God, once we start to redraw or even *remove* the boundaries of God, there's no knowing where we might end up! To lose control in this way is more than most people (and certainly most bishops) can bear (see Chapter 17). Perhaps the size of the God a person worships relates directly to the breadth of her mind and the depth of her imagination? The wider her horizons the less she will want to try to define and delimit this God: and vice versa.

The religious quest can be summed up as the attempt to distinguish God from the idols. This means that each individual's journey is going to be a continual movement from one less-than-adequate idea of God to the next: and so on, indefinitely. It's easy to mistake religious idols for the real thing; it happens all the time. Idols may be user-friendly, they may be readily available and accessible, they may come accompanied by catchy tunes and smiling faces. But if they make us want to linger, the chances are they're not the real thing: the journey to God is one that always urges us onward. The essence of the God-symbol (and to call it a symbol is not to limit the range of ways of understanding it: both theists and non-theists would accept that the word 'God' is a symbol, a pointer, whose function is to direct our attention elsewhere) is to keep reminding us that there is *always* more to reality than we currently think; it is a way of keeping us open to new understandings and new perspectives. The sacred, the truly holy, is *always* out of our reach, *always* inciting and inviting us to continue journeying. To feel that we have reached the terminus is to call a halt at what is just a religious mirage: there *is* no terminus, only a lifelong journey. Wisdom is always a goal, always an aspiration; there can never be a point when someone could sensibly say that they'd 'arrived': to live *is* to explore, in each and every way.

Those who talk most about God tend to be those who have most idolised God. If we really *do* want to enlarge the image/concept/idea (none of the words is adequate) of God, and move from the God-idol to something genuinely God-like, we may need to stop thinking of God as another 'thing' (albeit a very special one) and begin thinking of God as a *symbol* or a *metaphor*, a way of pointing to everything we consider to be of absolute meaning and value for us, a way of indicating something of the depth and mystery at the very heart of human life. Most Christians are able to think of God as being a separate 'existent', but many outside the Church, as well as some of those inside, find the notion very problematic. They might find it more helpful to think instead of the sort of meanings that can be attached to the God-symbol, such as what do we give ourselves to without reservation?

To focus on the *word* 'God', and make its use into a sort of touchstone of religious seriousness, is in fact to be *doubly* idolatrous. It's bad enough to make God into an idol: it's even worse to make the *word* 'God' into an idol as well! Idolatry is characterised (at least at a conscious level) by a sense of security and certainty, which often expresses itself in torrents of words. This is hardly surprising, given the clarity with which many orthodox believers understand their faith. But if people felt brave enough to leave the idols behind, and to move away from the security of traditional ideas, it's likely that words would rapidly begin to seem inadequate. 'Negative' (or 'apophatic') theology recognises the impossibility of saying anything substantive about God, and to indicate this perhaps the word 'God' needs to be written in a special way (for example with lines through it: ~~God~~). As soon as words are spoken about 'God' (rather than '~~God~~') idolatry is just around the corner because words 'objectify' (and therefore limit) the things to which they refer.

We live in a noisy, clamorous, unreflective world, and it would be good if the Church had the confidence and the reverence to offer something rather different, instead of contributing its own form of incessant babble. Many people fear silence (see Chapter 25) because it forces them to confront all manner of troubling thoughts and issues. The more idol-like is the God that people worship, the more noise they

Chapter 28

THINKING ABOUT FUNDAMENTALISM

Probably the main reason for thinking about Fundamentalism is because it's on the increase in many parts of the world, and can be pretty scary. It's the result of the interplay between fear and simple-mindedness, and has the great appeal that it absolves its adherents from having to think for themselves. Christian Fundamentalist churches are growing fast, with their particular attraction being to those who aren't able or don't want to ask questions. Being part of Fundamentalist religion is like going on the ultimate package holiday: everything is taken care of and all that's required is for you to do what you're told. Your views are neither asked for, nor wanted. There's no possibility of being selective: you buy into the whole package, or leave it all alone.

Christian Fundamentalism is less than a century old, and grew up in response to the perceived threats of biblical criticism and science, particularly Darwin's Theory of Evolution. It took its name from a series of pamphlets entitled *The Fundamentals of the Faith,* published by a group of American conservative Evangelicals between 1910-15, which set out what their authors claimed were 'the primary Christian themes'. In addition to the virgin birth and the physical resurrection, these included a belief in the Second Coming of Jesus and a view of scripture as the literal Word of God. This last one is the foundation of all the rest: the Bible is regarded as inerrant and complete; it is accepted as having absolute authority, and its words are the standard by which all values and behaviour are to be judged.

Contemporary scholars have challenged each of these claims, but this simply makes those who hold them even more determined to cling on to what they see as the essentials of the faith. It's an approach which cannot be reconciled with rational enquiry, because it admits no possibility of being mistaken: no evidence could be brought which would show the claims of Fundamentalism to be false, and this in itself indicates that, despite appearances to the contrary, it is making no truth claims at all. Of course, anyone is entitled to engage in make-believe or play fantasy games, and when children do this it is seen as a normal and entirely harmless part of growing up. The problem only comes when the growth process is arrested, and adults continue to indulge themselves in this way.

Unfortunately the closed and anti-rational mind-set of the Fundamentalists has considerable appeal, and enormous numbers of books of this persuasion are published. Bookshops with the word 'Christian' in their name are likely to be stocked mainly, if not exclusively with such anti-intellectual productions, and anyone venturing into them would go away with the idea that Christianity is a strange and rather sad phenomenon. In addition, the way in which the political Right (especially in America) has formed an unholy alliance with Fundamentalism gives intelligent outsiders yet another good reason to steer well clear of Christianity.

The outlook of Fundamentalists is a result of the interplay of certainty and fear. On the surface, *certainty* that their ways of thinking are right; but at a deeper level perhaps *fear* that they might not be. The only way to quell those fears is to try and silence those who dare to explore and challenge – a classic case of shooting the messenger. Such insularity can only operate inside religious ghettoes, where a siege-mentality develops on the part of the inmates who set up their own schools, colleges and publishing houses, as well as radio and television stations. The main purpose of these is not to evangelise those outside, but to reassure those inside. This is because the more you can associate with people who see the world in the way that you do, the more confidence you can have in that particular perspective. Indeed, the less it seems to *be* a perspective, and the more it seems to be simply the way things are. The result of this is that even when such people have considerable political power, their worldview remains small-minded and both backward- and inward-looking.

Relatively few people in this country would call themselves Fundamentalists, but considerable numbers would call themselves Evangelicals. Although there are important differences between them, many Evangelicals favour an understanding of the Bible that is more literalistic than critical, confident in their ability to get to unadulterated biblical truth: 'nothing added, nothing taken away', in the words of the old advertising slogan for shredded wheat. To religious liberals (see Chapter 18) the idea that it's possible to read the Bible (see Chapter 2) in this way is ludicrous, of course; but there are significant numbers of people who are convinced that when they read it, they really *are* getting a transcript of God's intentions for the world. It is salutary (and frightening) to note that 45% of Americans subscribe to the Creationist view that the world is only some 8000 years old.

Fundamentalists are clear about all sorts of things: in fact, seeing the world in black-and-white terms is at the very heart of the Fundamentalist perspective. Sexual matters loom large in their minds, and they are particularly exercised by abortion and homosexuality, both of which they find abhorrent. They would like traditional gender roles to be re-established; divorce to be made more difficult; Creationism to be given at least equal status in schools with the Theory of Evolution; more money spent on defence and law and order (they are often strong advocates of armed intervention overseas together with capital punishment at home) and less on the welfare state; a greater role for market forces and a reduction in government regulations. The clarity of the Fundamentalist vision has considerable appeal: many of its supporters are prepared to give freely of their time and money, with tithing being widely practised. This contrasts with those church members who can manage with much less religion in their lives, and who have very different personal priorities.

There are many ways of looking at the world, and the one we end up with is probably more a matter of psychology than reason. The fact that Fundamentalism is not simply an approach to a collection of ancient texts, but typically also involves a particular set of attitudes towards a whole range of issues, lends support to this idea. It shows that we *don't* come to a view as to the historicity or otherwise of the Bible in an objective way; our attitude to it is the result of a mind-set that tends towards either certainty or scepticism on all sorts of matters. The liberal's doubts about what lies behind biblical texts are likely to be part of an openness towards sexual mores, and a willingness to empathise with the poor and the dispossessed, which will probably express itself in a wish to regulate the tendency of the market to drive wages and working conditions downwards.

It's not surprising that the anti-intellectualism at the heart of much popular culture finds a religious expression in Fundamentalism. The clarity of vision that results means that people may feel able to dispense with the immense effort required to think through religious and ethical issues, and simply acquire an off-the-peg worldview. Probably every generation looks back with nostalgia to the golden age of their youth, and the popularity of old films (especially old war films) supports this idea. The past is safe, because it's unchanging; it can't spring any unpleasant surprises on us. No matter if the view of the past that sustains us lacks historicity: a belief that summers used to be hotter is enough. Religion is a source of support for many, and Fundamentalism does this particularly well by taking people back to a time when certainties really were certainties. No matter that they weren't, no matter that things were immensely more complicated than this: it is enough that the vision is communicated. Fundamentalism offers security, something that many people desperately crave. To the extent that it helps keep troubled souls afloat it is to be commended, in that drowning people need life jackets rather than swimming lessons. But given that its origins are fear and its lifeblood is ignorance, it cannot be seen as something that helps human flourishing.

In addition, the feeling of certainty that is part of Fundamentalism can lead to a dangerous intolerance. This is because a sense of being on God's side can result in people behaving towards others in ways that they otherwise wouldn't dream of doing. Mild-mannered men and women can become transformed into religious maniacs if they are sufficiently convinced of the rightness of their cause. Fundamentalists (whether political or religious) are always potential menaces, because their sense of oneness with what is essentially a tribal God, means that they feel able to reject all those who are not members of the tribe. The sense of belonging which such fierce tribal identity provides, and which is so gratefully latched on to by the inadequate and the lost, is seen in lesser form in the violence of football hooligans, and in fully developed form in the suicide bombers. Fundamentalism provides an anchor in a world that to some seems to be falling apart, with its plethora of values (many of them considered alien) and no clear guiding principles to hold everything together. Fundamentalism is thus *both* a part of the postmodern flux (see Chapter 21) *and* a desperate protest against it.

Chapter 29

THINKING ABOUT THE TRINITY

During the 1980s and 1990s, Britain's Labour Party came to terms with the reality that it could either be a socialist party of opposition, or it could ditch a lot of its dogma, and stand a chance of being elected. This led to a great deal of soul-searching, because those who were keenest on the socialist ideology tended also to be those who were keenest to help the poor in all sorts of practical ways – something they couldn't do all the while they remained out of government. The modernisers won, the Party embraced pragmatism, and swept into power. Some say that they sold out; others that they saw sense.

Christianity in modern Britain is at a comparable crossroads. It can continue in the same way that it has been doing for centuries and hope for the best, or it can take seriously the fact that it is haemorrhaging members, and admit that its plight is so dire that desperate remedies are called for. The Labour Party became electable once it stopped frightening people: the concern among many voters was that the hard-line Socialists were poised to take over, and such a prospect did not have mass appeal. Similarly, there is concern among many people that within the Church hard-line Fundamentalists and fellow believers are in the ascendancy, which means that there is no welcome and no place for those who see things differently. Until those worries are addressed many of those outside will remain there, becoming increasingly desperate at their lack of a spiritual home.

The Church, like the Labour Party has lots of dogmas, lots of ideas that define the sort of organisation that it is. It cannot simply abandon them, because they are the things that give it an identity, they are the things that make it what it is. But it can look at those ideas and see whether they might be understood more generously, perhaps more *creatively*. Unless it does this, it will continue to be a sort of principled irrelevance to most people in the country, incapable of helping them make sense of their lives, and condemned to become an ever more inward-looking sect.

The Trinity is one of the central dogmas of Christianity, and it's worth looking to see if its ideas could be understood in ways that help rather than hinder the Church's attempts to be a transforming influence in society. Jesus, of course, had never heard of the Trinity, and this was because the idea didn't get invented until hundreds of years after his death. In many ways it's a product of its times, of the way that people thought and argued in the 4th century. And although it's had a long and honourable career, it *can* be a positive stumbling block to the Gospel. Christianity often appears to require people to believe things which are at best tricky, and at worst impossible – and the doctrine of the Trinity stands out head and shoulders above the rest in terms of testing to the limit our ability to believe something that sounds like a logical contradiction. How *can* something be, at the same time, one *and* three things, one *and* three **persons**?

People don't *discover* doctrines, of course, but *invent* them. And they do this, not to make life more difficult but to make it easier. Doctrines are invented to deal with particular problems, and so it is with the doctrine of the Trinity. The problem started with the story of the Incarnation, the idea that in Jesus, God came to earth. But this immediately raised the question of whether God was any longer 'in heaven'? If God became human, was there anything 'left' of the divinity of God? Is God completely on earth, or is there a sort of *residue* still in heaven? And if we address Jesus as God, is there anyone else, any other *bit* of God, to address?

It really boils down to the question, how many Gods are there: one or two? And what sense, if any, can we make of the idea that Jesus was 'fully Man *and* fully God'? It was thought essential that there was 'enough' God in Jesus – because a Jesus who was human *and nothing more* was not one that appealed to many of the Church Fathers. Hardly surprisingly, this whole question was thrashed around for centuries, and it was complicated further by the fact that the earliest Christian tradition also speaks about God's Spirit as a Person, and so a place had to be found for this as well.

The doctrine of the Trinity therefore grew up as a way of dealing with the most intractable theological questions that faced the early Church. The claim is that there is one divine *substance*, which consists of the three 'persons' of Father, Son and Holy Spirit, and although this became the core of Christian doctrine, for most Christians now it probably means little and matters less. The doctrine was born from the interplay between early Christianity and Greek philosophy. But philosophy, like all subjects, moves on, and old ideas are either discarded, or at least substantially reworked. And because the idea of 'substance', which so intrigued the Greek philosophers is no longer a live issue, the Trinity is in danger of becoming a sort of fossil on the beach of the history of ideas. This isn't to say that it's not important: but it *is* to say that it needs to be re-examined, and if necessary reinterpreted, so that it can continue to operate as a central Christian symbol.

When we talk about 'Ultimate Reality' or 'Ultimate Mystery' we're not talking about some 'object', or 'thing'; neither are we just uttering empty words. We're speaking poetically, not scientifically; we're giving voice, inevitably inadequately and clumsily, to that sense of awe and wonder and cosmic puzzlement which lies at the heart of the whole religious impulse. And the first 'person' of the Trinity is a way of underpinning our religious discourse with the sense of mystery that is so crucial. But if that's all there is, then the concept of God would be empty: Ultimate Mystery doesn't lead us anywhere, because its very lack of content means that there's nothing we can, so to speak, 'get hold of'. And this is why the other two parts of the doctrine of the Trinity are so important.

As Christians, we think of Jesus as 'the human face of God', and this means that we find focussing on his teaching and example gives us insight into what is most really real – into Ultimate Reality, if you like. And because 'God' is another name for Ultimate Reality, it means that Jesus gives us a window into God. God the Son, in the form of the incarnate Jesus, provides the model and the example that we need.

But because Jesus is no longer on earth, the way in which we can think of him continuing is through the medium of the Holy Spirit. This third 'person' of the Trinity expresses the understanding that God is everywhere, at all times and in all places. And shows that there is no radical separation between the secular and the sacred, but only one reality.

The doctrine of the Trinity, with its blending of diversity in unity, is a way of expressing the insight of faith that, despite appearances, everything is part of a single whole. There are not two realms, one sacred and one secular, but a unity – the three 'aspects' of the One being different facets, different points of view of reality. To say 'there is only one God' means that reality is one and undivided. It's not a case of thinking that each of the three parts of the Trinity can somehow 'exist' by themselves – that would make no more sense than thinking that each side of a triangle can, somehow, have an existence independent of the other two.

There's always the danger, especially in an increasingly secular age, that Christianity will get reduced to being simply a code of ethics. People may call themselves Christians because they more-or-less follow Christian moral teachings, but if that's all there is, then to claim that they're Christians is to misuse the language. Christianity is (and requires) a great deal more, and although following an ethical code is *necessary* to being a Christian, it is by no means *sufficient*. And this is brought out very well by the doctrine of the Trinity, with its foundation being God the Father. This is the bedrock of everything, and provides the 'numinousness' or 'otherness', which is at the heart of genuine religion.

But what can we *do* with all this? Unlike, say, one of the parables, there are no obvious implications for action. But in fact it is of the most enormous importance, because the very *incomprehensibility* of the Trinity stops us from feeling that we've ever got God all sewn up. We say the Nicene Creed at Communion services, whilst the Apostles Creed is said at Mattins and Evensong. But the Athanasian Creed is never said at all, for very understandable reasons. One section speaks of 'The Father incomprehensible, the Son incomprehensible: and the Holy Ghost incomprehensible', and a little later adds that 'as also there are not three incomprehensibles, nor three uncreated: but one uncreated and one incomprehensible'. It's hardly surprising that people avoid this stuff, regarding the *whole thing* as incomprehensible – but it does point to the vital truth that God (Ultimate Reality, if you prefer) is beyond *anything* we can make sense of. It also shows up the fatuity of the matey, God-as-a-nice-bloke speak which is so often found in contemporary Church circles. This contrasts with a sense of the fearful holiness of Ultimate Mystery that is part of grown-up religion, and which takes us directly into the land of the wordless, the land where the only appropriate response is silence and awe (see Chapter 25).

Of course, someone might, very reasonably, ask how we can distinguish between something incomprehensible *and profound* – and something incomprehensible *and ridiculous*. Rather than getting involved in metaphysics, the key consideration is what difference, if any, the idea in question makes to our lives. The doctrine of the Trinity should help us guard against the banal in our worship, the simplistic in our thinking, and the complacent in our living. And therefore, whatever ontological status the Trinity may have, there's more than enough justification for us to continue taking it seriously.

Chapter 30

THINKING ABOUT LITURGY

Liturgy is what goes on in church services, and the language used is crucial, because in addition to setting the tone of the occasion, it also reflects and shapes the religious understanding of the participants. This is why liturgy and theology need to go hand in hand.

Theology (see Chapter 17), like all areas of human thought, is always developing, with new insights being taken on board, and older, less helpful ones discarded. And although fewer and fewer people in the western world are involved in organised religion, the *reflection on* religion that is theology is alive and well. One of the most important theological developments of recent years has been the increasing number of people who have rejected the theistic idea of God (see Chapter 1) in favour of a post-theistic model. The God of theism has had a good innings, and indeed for most people represents the only way of thinking about God that they have ever come across. It is the theistic idea of God that those who want nothing to do with religion are rejecting, just as it tends to be the theistic idea of God that those who are very much involved in religion are attached to. This picture understands God as a personal being, all-powerful, all-knowing and all-present. Such a God is the creator and sustainer of the universe, with no cause, no beginning and no end. He is beyond thought and the only way that we can respond to him is by constant praise and worship.

It is a picture that more and more people have found less and less plausible, and unless alternative ways of thinking about God are offered, fewer and fewer intelligent people will be able to take Christianity seriously. This is such an awful prospect that everyone who is convinced of the value of Christianity is bound to want to do everything they can to try and ensure that the faith they so treasure can remain open and available to all those who are seriously interested in exploring the religious dimension of human life. Given that it is the theistic God that is the major stumbling block for so many, it follows that this is something that needs addressing as a matter of urgency.

Unfortunately, it is only the theistic God who makes an appearance in church services, and so anyone wandering in may easily go away with the idea that this is the only way both of being religious and doing theology. Given that most people get involved in religion before they get involved in theology, it means that attention needs to be given to the language and concepts used in the liturgy to reflect the developments made in theology, so that we are no longer constrained by a way of thinking about God which, for many, has passed its sell-by date.

Liturgy is a human invention, just as all words used about God (or anything else) are human inventions. Anyone who takes Christianity seriously would agree that God is the most profound idea that human beings can ever grapple with. This means that all words used are inadequate – but some are more inadequate than others. For many, the theistic God has become an idol (see Chapter 27) and it is important for them, as well as for all those who cannot do anything whatsoever with this idea, to consider other possibilities.

The problem is that the very limitations of the theistic God are also its attractions. He/She is essentially a human being writ very large, with all our positive qualities expanded to an infinite degree, and all our negative qualities taken out. Because we can relate to each other, we can, analogously, make sense of the idea of relating to such a God – and this is the case even if we don't believe that this kind of God actually exists! But if we move beyond such an idea, everything becomes very problematic and uncertain. And although such exploration may mean that we are being far more open and honest about the profound Mystery of God, it also makes it impossible for us to get our minds around him and the whole thing becomes a lot less user-friendly.

Such a shift means moving from seeing God as a *being* to seeing God as a *symbol*; from seeing God as *transcendent* (outside us) to seeing God as *immanent* (inside us). It involves seeing God as the power of Love as expressed in community, God as the well-spring of joyful, exuberant living and giving. There's no question of urging people to abandon the theistic model, if that still retains its power to help them grow in love. Rather, it's about offering another picture, which they may find adds a further dimension to their worship, and may help others to engage in worship for the first time. It's not a matter of one picture being right and another wrong, but of one picture helping some people, and another picture helping others. Only the most blinkered and bigoted (and indeed selfish) will find themselves unable to welcome the offering of *additional* perspectives and pictures that could provide a means for those currently outside the churches to find a way in!

'God' is the name we give to the eternally elusive, eternally profound Mystery at the heart of human life; the thing that art and music and poetry try to point towards. It would be absurd (and probably blasphemous) to try and limit this in terms of particular labels and concepts. Religious conservatives may say that the post-theist has lost her faith but this would simply show their own deep personal limitations. What has happened is that the post-theist has *moved deeper into the mystery of faith*, and has had to coin new metaphors and tell new stories as a result.

These need to be reflected in new liturgies because it is in and through liturgy that we engage with the Mystery at the heart of everything. Instead of the cringing, self-obeisance which is at the centre of so many church services, we need to find ways to celebrate the glory of human life, the power and wonder of human love, and the importance of making the most of each and every new day.

If we move beyond theism it means people no longer need to think of God as a being with many of the less attractive features of a tribal overlord (including such capriciousness that unless constantly pleaded with, he/she is liable to send diseases and other misfortunes in a seemingly cavalier way). It would also relieve them of the burden of trying to make literal sense of intercessory prayer (see Chapter 4). Liturgies would need to reflect a new maturity as people found ways of taking responsibility for their lives, moving beyond the quest for certainty and security, fully aware of the exhilarating riskiness of the everyday and joyfully and courageously embracing the unknown. The new liturgies would need to reflect the shift from Power to Love, because the theistic God helped underpin all manner of brutal persecutions, and even today continues to undergird patriarchy, racism, homophobia and global capitalism.

Liturgy matters because God matters. The sort of God we worship says a lot about the sort of people we are, and the sort of world we want to help build, but unless our liturgy reflects our religious aspirations, unless it gives voice to what is really important to us, it is failing to do what it's there for. We are called to break down barriers between the secular and the sacred, between believers and non-believers, between male and female, between straight and gay, and so on. This means taking each others' needs and pains with as much seriousness and tenderness as we can muster and, rather than thinking in terms of religious uniformity and orthodoxy, focusing on genuinely disinterested acts of giving.

However, few of these ideas and ideals are reflected in our hymns and prayers which continue to beg and plead with God, to praise and flatter, to cower and grovel. We still pray and sing about Jesus dying on the Cross 'for our sins', 'as a sacrificial victim', something which was needed if God (understood as a sort of despot) was to forgive and forget the business in the Garden of Eden. Many have no problems with any of this, either because they have a very literal turn of mind or because they are able to understand it all in a metaphorical or poetic sense. But there are plenty of others who are unable to perform the requisite mental gymnastics, and who come to the conclusion that this stuff really isn't for them.

New liturgies may be more celebratory than penitential, more communal than individual in their emphasis, more concerned with bringing healing and wholeness to communities, nations, even the planet, than with personal soul-saving. There will be more of a focus upon the things we can (and ought to) do, rather than trying to persuade a theistic God to do them on our behalf. Sin (see Chapter 32), although undoubtedly terribly real, needs to be given far less prominence. The old view saw marriage as 'a remedy against sin', baptism as necessary because 'men are conceived and born in sin', illness as punishment for sin, and death as a blessed release from sin ('man that is born of a woman hath but a short time to live, and is full of misery'). All of these are sad and sick, and show the extent to which human life was seen not as something wonderful that needed to be celebrated but as something depraved which needed to be apologised for. Things have changed in recent years, but there's a long way to go – and major liturgical reform is needed to help speed the pace.

Our liturgies contain genuinely powerful words and ideas, and the riches of many of the 1662 services are particularly to be treasured. They don't need to be abandoned, but demythologised, which means interpreting and even re-imagining them, so that those who take part in the services realise the range of possible ways of understanding what is said and done. It's not a matter of 'not meaning' the words, but of 'meaning' a whole lot more than meets the eye. But the problem remains that many of those who hear the words may not realise that they *can* be understood in a non-literal sense. New liturgies are therefore needed to help open up the understanding of God, and to point people towards ways of entering the Mystery more creatively and profoundly.

New liturgies will obviously continue to focus on the Bible (see Chapter 2) but will also supplement its words with those of more recent writers. It would be absurd to suggest that nothing of value has been produced since the canon of scripture was closed, and the range of prose and poetry available is almost limitless. Above all, the new liturgies will have a new emphasis on the *search* for truth, rather than implying that the last word has been said. The story goes on – with and through us.

so leads to all sorts of philosophical and theological difficulties. Conservative Christians such as Fundamentalists seem particularly prone to talking about the 'power of evil', seeing it as having a sort of independent existence (perhaps it does, but unless and until other explanations fail, it's much safer *not* to assume this to be the case). Some conservative Christians take part in rites aimed at driving out ('exorcising') the 'evil spirits' (an even more problematic concept) that are thought to 'inhabit' particular places or people (see Chapter 24). This is a way of looking at the world that raises as many questions about the state of mind of those who seek to effect a 'cure' in this way as of those thought to be 'possessed'.

Evil can be thought of as extreme moral wrong, and is often concerned with power: the wish to dominate and control another person. Although it may be expressed in horribly dramatic forms, the people involved may be very ordinary. Many serial killers are unexceptional, even dull people, whilst completely law-abiding citizens can have a coldness about them that expresses itself in such complete indifference to the needs of others that they might also be thought of as having significant evil potential. It's salutary to note that the systematic destruction of the human spirit almost certainly takes place more often within respectable homes than within torture cells, and shows how evil is both widespread and very ordinary.

Institutionalised evil comes in all sorts of guises: Hitler's Germany, Stalin's Russia, Pol Pot's Cambodia, Amin's Uganda, Verwoerd's South Africa. Whatever monsters may have been in charge, each of these systems depended on ordinary, decent people to keep it all working. This in turn suggests that many (perhaps most? maybe even all?) ordinary, decent people have the potential for evil, if the circumstances are propitious. Evil is what can happen when the normal social and psychological restraints are removed, because it is then that the darkest and cruellest aspects of the human personality can be unleashed. There is no need to think of evil forces being abroad, out *there*, in the world: there are more than enough within ourselves to be going on with. But because this is a pretty uncomfortable idea, many think of evil as something 'other', rather than simply part of the normal human condition. And in the same way that lots of people find it comforting to pass the responsibility for their lives to an all-powerful deity, many also find it helpful to project all the dark forces within themselves on to an external 'devil'. This is particularly the case with those who are deeply disturbed, or Fundamentalists (see Chapter 28), or both.

The reification of evil, by objectifying it and locating it somewhere other than within ourselves, can lead to all sorts of problems. Unless we are able to accept our own dark side, with all its blemishes, we will tend to be super-critical of others, projecting on them the self-hatred that we dare not acknowledge. But if we are able to see evil as what happens when the human spirit expresses itself in ways that are socially unacceptable, that realisation can help give us a sense of humility. Learning to accept ourselves, nasty bits and all, is the best possible antidote to a sense of smugness and self-importance, things which often discourage those outside the Church from setting foot inside.

But just as objectifying evil causes problems, the same thing happens when God is reified/objectified, especially when people put together the idea of a world which clearly contains evil, and a God who is traditionally thought of as all-loving and all-powerful. This is known as the 'Problem of Evil', a term that should not be confused with the 'problem of evil'. The latter is a brute fact about the world we live in, a world in which people suffer in all sorts of ways. This painful reality challenges us to try and improve things, so that the amount of suffering is reduced to an absolute minimum. The 'Problem of Evil', on the other hand, is a theological rather than a practical matter, and provides conventional religious believers with the intellectual problem of trying to hang on to their conception of God. The use of Ockham's Razor provides a way out of this difficulty, by reminding us that the 'Problem' only exists on the basis of certain assumptions. And although they are very widely held, the fact that they *are* assumptions means that a different starting point will lead to a very different conclusion.

The Holocaust marked a turning point in the way that many people thought about God. After Auschwitz, it was widely held that belief in an omnipotent, loving God was no longer possible: how *could* such a God have watched and not acted? The attempt to show how belief is still an option in such circumstances is called 'theodicy'. There are many strands to it, one of the key ones focusing on the idea of human free will. Much of the suffering in the world is due not to the curiously named 'acts of God' (plagues, famines, earthquakes, etc) but to deliberate human intent (wars, ethnic cleansing, etc). It is said that because we are free to choose how to behave, given that we are surrounded by temptations of all sorts (and given further that temptation, by definition, is only ever to do what we know to be wrong: it makes little sense to say that I was tempted last Thursday to be kind!) there are likely to be many occasions when people choose to behave in ways that are morally wrong. If the consequences of such actions are sufficiently awful (the result perhaps of a lack of a sense of morality, or a condition of insanity) they might be said to be 'evil', and the term may also be used of those who carried them out.

The suggestion that we alone are responsible for our actions, and that God shouldn't take any of the blame, is met by the observation that people behave as they do, because they are as they are: and it's God who has made them like that. Would it have been possible for such a God to create human beings who had free will (itself a very tricky notion) and who always employed it to choose courses of action that resulted in pleasure not pain? But perhaps a world without evil would also be a world without good, because unless there were bad alternatives, there couldn't be good alternatives. If so, it means that moral choice depends on the existence of unpleasant consequences; and therefore a perfectly good world (or a heaven?) could not be in any sense a *moral* world.

As with all arguments, where you end up depends on where you start. The people who are desperate to preserve their faith intact may, by judicious selection of premises, manage to do so. Those for whom faith is impossible may well find their view reinforced as a result of the premises that they (unconsciously) adopt. Once again it shows that assumptions (premises) are everything: there is no perspective-less position, no 'view-from-nowhere', and we need to be open (with ourselves as much as anyone) about how a great deal of theology is a matter of trying to find reasons to continue thinking in the way that we already do, rather than trying to advance our understanding of things.

Much of theology is concerned with trying to deal with obstacles to faith: if someone finds lots of things standing in the way, and if they really *do* want to be able to engage with religion, they may be prepared to put in the time and effort necessary. People for whom such obstacles don't exist, or who don't have any interest in religion, may well do no theological thinking whatsoever. The Problem of Evil constitutes such an obstacle for many people, but only because God is usually thought of as an independent being who is both All Good and All Powerful. Remove any of those three assumptions and the Problem disappears – but so does the God of conventional Christianity! And although the Problem of Evil raises all sorts of difficulties, and although the use of Ockham's Razor provides a means of dealing with it, the way that it *also* cuts away at the theistic concept of God is likely to be seen as so deeply threatening and disturbing that many people may do the equivalent of pulling the bedclothes up over their heads to make it all go away.

Chapter 32

THINKING ABOUT SIN

Given the slightest excuse we romanticise the past. Money went further, the summers were hotter, the children better behaved, the neighbours were friendlier. Maybe, maybe not – but there's something suspicious about the fact that every generation seems to think like this! Religion is full of such embellishing of history: in the past the churches were fuller, the people more God-fearing, and religious truth was beyond dispute. And of course, if we only go back far enough, there was, literally, heaven-on-earth. God created everything in a state of perfection, and human beings came along and spoiled it. As always, it only needed one person to ruin it for the rest, and it remained like this until God sent Jesus to clear up the mess. Atonement is the view that Jesus managed this by taking upon himself all the sins (past, present, and presumably future) of the human race and offering himself in the same sort of way that sacrificial lambs were offered to God in the centuries before Jesus was born.

It's a repulsive picture, based upon a monstrous understanding of God. And although it might just be possible to make sense of it as something that was believed in simpler, more primitive times, the fact that considerable numbers of Christians continue to subscribe to it today is very scary indeed. Not only does it reinforce the idea of Christianity as being unspeakably ludicrous, but it also gives such a high priority to sin that it threatens to distort the entire Christian message. These ideas are given voice in phrases such as 'Jesus died for my sins' and as a result I am 'washed in the blood of the Lamb', language that is grotesque and disgusting to most intelligent and civilised people. Unlike people of two or more millennia ago, we don't live in a culture where blood sacrifice is practised, and shudder at the primitive superstitiousness of it all.

The writings of St Paul and St Augustine, with their emphasis on the congenital wickedness of everyone, have meant that from the very birth of the Christian story, sin has been at the centre, with human beings seen as so depraved, so sin-full, that without divine help they would be utterly lost. But there's something not just grotesque but deeply offensive about the idea of each newborn baby already contaminated by the stain of Original Sin. Most thoughtful people would see this as bizarre and horrible, and need to be reassured that not only is it not necessary for them to adopt such a notion in order to be a Christian, but that they would in fact be far better off without it.

The emphasis on sin has meant that Christianity has come to be seen as life-*denying* rather than life-*enhancing*; as a miserable, guilt-ridden, disapproving way of looking at the world, indeed perhaps the most negative view of human nature of any religion. This in turn has meant that people were traditionally regarded as holy if they kept themselves untainted by the world, through having as little contact with it as possible. Particular exception was taken by the faithful to sins of the flesh, and this is no surprise given that sex is *the* expression of life's self-affirmation. Holiness was seen as sexlessness, with celibacy being viewed as far superior to sensuality. There may be a measure of self-hatred in all this, with many people so uneasy with their own sexual drive and nature that they feel obliged to adopt an attitude of tight-lipped disapproval in order to try and keep a lid on the whole thing.

St Paul's view was that there was no need for someone to do lots of bad things in order to count as sinful: however good, however kind, however self-giving someone is makes no difference at all. As a result of Adam's behaviour (understood by Augustine in a literal sense, and, tragically and embarrassingly, all too often *still* understood in that way) sin was introduced to the world – and, like an incurable infectious disease, has been endemic ever since. Every single person is born, lives and dies in a state of sin, indeed is riddled with it. This is hardly surprising given both the ubiquitousness of sexual desire and the disgust that it engendered in many of those who were responsible for formulating the teachings of the Early Church.

This is a sad, sick, stupid view of life, and the sooner it disappears the better. Of course there are countless examples of people doing all sorts of terrible things to one another, but these are only part of the story, and need to be set alongside the far more common examples of people behaving decently, sometimes even heroically. The supposed perfection of creation stemmed, at least in part, from the idea that God made it all according to a specific design. Darwin and the cosmologists have shown that the work of creation goes on, and that far from everything going downhill, things are very much on the up, as organisms become increasingly complex and better adapted to their surroundings. The idea of Atonement follows on naturally from that of 'The Fall', but if many people no longer find the latter at all persuasive or helpful then they are likely to have no time for the former either.

An alternative picture might be 'The Ascent', focusing on how, at the individual level, each human being is capable of personal moral growth, whilst at the collective level, the spread of democracies together with the increasing unacceptability of discrimination against ethnic minorities or women or homosexuals, shows that real improvements have been made. Of course dreadful savagery still goes on, often religious in origin, whilst within more stable societies there are innumerable ways in which we could do even better. But at least by starting on the basis that people are fundamentally decent, albeit ignorant or incomplete or indeed damaged, a much more positive, optimistic tone is struck. 'The Ascent' is as much a myth as 'The Fall', but one that is life-affirming rather than life-denying.

Instead of focusing on the potential for doing harm that is in each of us, 'The Ascent' dwells on our potential for doing good. Many people in our society have a low self-image, and this tends to express itself in all sorts of antisocial ways. There is a very real danger of making things worse if Christians go around stressing how wicked and worthless we all are. The reality is that we *are* constantly making mistakes, constantly making the wrong choices. But this certainly doesn't make us all wicked, and if sadly earnest Christians insist on applying the word 'wicked' to everyone, we will need to invent a new word to refer to those who are what the rest of society means when they use the term. We are weak, we are ignorant, we are careless, and each of these can have terribly unfortunate consequences. But instead of proclaiming that we are hopelessly 'fallen creatures', it would be much better to say that we are able to use our lack of wholeness in either a creative or a destructive way.

'Sin' is essentially a religious term, and tends only to be used ironically outside the context of religion. To feel sinful is to feel wretched in the sight of God, that is by comparison with an Absolute moral standard. Sin is conventionally seen as the breaking of the rules of life that have been laid down by God, and so those who have moved beyond the God of theism (see Chapters 1 and 30) are bound to think of sin in a different way as well. The essence of sin is failure, something that is as common and as natural as breathing. We fail to *be* all that we should and we fail to *do* all that we should. We fail to love other people, we fail to take them seriously, we fail to be open to their ideas and insights, we fail to embrace life and exist in a pinched, self-centred way. There are simply *so many ways* that we get things wrong, and this is why we can never do without the idea of sin. It is the inevitable accompaniment of a capacity for self-reflection and self-criticism, together with an essential reminder of the need to reverence the mystery at the heart of everything.

But although we cannot manage without the idea of sin, it is high time that it played a much less prominent role in Christianity, and we focused far more on the teachings of Jesus and less on those of more negative souls. Instead of the gross and embarrassing 'repent or burn' approach, we need more along the lines of 'love and flourish'. And although it is customary to lament the decline of Christianity in our society, as far as Open Christians are concerned, an end to the baleful dominance of the ideas about sin that stem from Paul and Augustine cannot come soon enough.

Chapter 33

THINKING ABOUT HEAVEN AND HELL

Most people probably give heaven and hell hardly any thought at all; and if they do it tends to be in terms of the ancient three-storey universe, with heaven above the earth and hell below it. They can't be blamed for thinking like this, of course, because that's what the Bible and the creeds seem to say. And indeed there *is* nothing wrong with thinking like this – so long as we don't try to apply such ideas *literally*. If we do, we end up with the sort of nonsense that has proved so effective at putting people off Christianity altogether.

Heaven is traditionally thought of as 'the place where God lives', which he shares with the angels, saints and chosen dead. Hell, on the other hand, is somewhere that is completely separated from God, and is the 'home of the Devil'. Going to hell, the place of endless punishment, was widely thought to be the fate of the wicked and the unbaptised, and fear of hell was (and to some extent, perhaps still is) an important agent of social control. Hymns, paintings, stained glass and poetry graphically depicted the waiting fires, and many people (especially the gullible and the simple) were presumably suitably chastened as a result. But hell today has little hold over anyone, and tends to be mentioned only in jokes. Civilised adults don't make jokes about truly painful subjects, and because jokes about hell are not thought to be on the edge of acceptability it shows that hell has, for almost everyone, lost its horrors.

Apart from Fundamentalists and some Evangelicals hell no longer matters because it is no longer taken seriously.

It is against this background that the Ascension of Jesus into Heaven remains for many one of the embarrassments of the Church year. Proclaimed loudly (and sometimes pictorially as well) on the notice boards outside churches, it means that passers-by are confronted with what seems to be yet *another* piece of evidence that Christians are either half-witted or insane. The impression given is that Jesus was an early astronaut, with the crucial difference being that unlike his immediate successor Yuri Gagarin, who returned to earth, Jesus simply kept on going. It's inevitable that the question as to whether he's still travelling will get asked: even from the most optimistic viewpoint, the 2000 light years he's been on the move means that he's barely even begun his journey across the Milky Way, which is itself an infinitesimal part of the universe as a whole. At this rate, it's going to be (literally) aeons before he gets to heaven!

To put it in those terms is to risk the wrath of the literalists, but it's worth doing because it shows the complete lunacy of thinking of Heaven as a *place*. In the days when little was known about the universe, such an idea may well have been reasonable: to hold it now is simply to invite ridicule. Heaven is not a place, hell is not a place: they are *spiritual* rather than physical realities. This doesn't mean they're not real, but it's the sort of reality explored by poets and painters and novelists, rather than cosmologists.

Although most people find the idea of hell-as-a-place completely incredible, they have far fewer problems with thinking of heaven in this way, even though they may be half aware of the difficulties already mentioned. Given that heaven is a much more attractive concept, this isn't perhaps surprising, but if we are trying to be consistent in our thinking it is still regrettable. In practice, the idea of heaven may amount to little more than a vague feeling that after death people (especially, but perhaps not exclusively those who lived 'good lives') continue to exist, but in a somehow 'better place'. It's particularly comforting to think this when trying to come to terms with the death of loved ones, or when contemplating one's own demise and hoped-for reunion with them. There's precious little empirical evidence to go on however, which means that holding this belief rather than simply being hopefully agnostic, is to invite accusations of wishful thinking.

Quite apart from these problems, the moral assumptions that underpin the idea of heaven and hell are to many both problematic and repugnant. Individual responsibility depends on freewill, but there are good reasons to suppose that at least some (and perhaps far more) of the actions that we carry out are constrained by circumstances and conditions entirely outside our control. If we cannot be said to be fully responsible, we cannot take either all the credit or all the blame. But without these there can be no possibility of judgement. And without *that* we can make no sense of the idea of there being a separation or grading of human beings at the point of death.

In addition to this problem, there is the fundamental difficulty about the kind of God who would be willing to inflict unimaginable torment on his creatures throughout the whole of eternity. Whatever the merits might be of punishment over a limited period, there can surely be no possible justification for *everlasting* punishment. But in the same way that public hangings and floggings were popular spectacles (and doubtless would be again, if they were provided) there are good reasons to think that many people (including Christians) derive considerable satisfaction from contemplating others 'getting their just deserts' – and if this goes on indefinitely, so be it. The idea of hell, in other words, has an unhealthy appeal to the baser instincts of disturbingly large numbers of people, and on these grounds alone its fading away would be welcome.

The traditional view of heaven or hell being our pay-off at the end of life, either reward or punishment as appropriate, rested on the idea of judgement, which in turn required a judge, God. The problem is that the sort of God involved, the God of theism (see Chapters 1 and

30) has come to seem less and less plausible to more and more people. A God who keeps a tally of each person's deeds, putting ticks and crosses against them, and entering them in a sort of celestial log book is seen by most adults as about as ludicrous as the idea of heaven being a place. But once the spatial dimension is removed, once we stop talking about supposedly physical things and move into the realm of spiritual realities, the whole thing starts to fall apart.

An example of this might be the idea of God 'reigning in heaven'. Understood literally it seems clear enough – but only until someone starts to think carefully about it, when it may begin to seem simply ridiculous. It doesn't have to, of course, but for far too long religion has been seen mainly, if not exclusively, in physical terms, which means that when the spiritual is taken seriously everything looks threateningly vague and insubstantial. Many people may indeed feel that attempting to think in this way is equivalent to undermining religion rather than an indication of spiritual maturity.

But in fact, if we take the spiritual seriously in this way, heaven and hell cease to be matters of speculation, and become actual and immediate. If we stop thinking of them as future states or places, and instead look on them as ways of understanding our everyday lives here and now, then heaven can be thought of as the state we are in when we are at peace, and hell the state we are in when we are in torment. This means that acting in ways that are destructive and hateful are guaranteed to put us in hell, whilst acting in ways that are constructive and loving can bring us to heaven, the realm of God. Such 'demythologising' means that heaven and hell are seen, not as metaphysical realities but as regulative ideals, to be understood not literally but figuratively and creatively.

The result is that although most people who reflect on heaven and hell and find the traditional picture, literally understood, so incoherent that they are unable to do anything with it, this can be seen not as a *problem* but as an *opportunity*. Far from meaning that heaven and hell are no longer important concepts, this may be just the spur needed to help people think more carefully about the relationship between the spatial and the spiritual, and in the process help them move beyond the idea of a theistic God. In turn this may make them more sympathetic to many of the problems that religious outsiders have with regards to Christianity, and in so doing may help it become a great deal more open and inclusive – and intelligent.

Chapter 34

THINKING ABOUT FORGIVENESS

'Forgive and forget' is very sound advice, but a lot easier said than done! To forgive someone is to wipe the slate clean and start again, just like repentance. Indeed, many people would say that forgiveness *requires* repentance, but it doesn't. However it *does* require imagination as well as the ability to empathise. It might also require mitigating circumstances, which reduce the culpability of the person – he did it because he had a troubled childhood, or because he's insane, or whatever.

Life operates on a ratchet, so there's never any possibility of going back. We can never undo things so as to have another go at the past: once something is done, it's done, and can never be *un*done. Forgiveness is the best we can manage in our attempt to make the best of what has gone wrong, which was why Jesus spoke so much about it, and indeed advocated forgiveness without limit. And although this may be seen as completely impractical, it unequivocally set the tone of his teaching. The baying mobs that gather outside courtrooms or around the front doors of supposed paedophiles show just how hard many people find it to do anything positive with their feelings of anger and repulsion (and this is so whether or not they are involved in religion). But it also shows how crucial forgiveness actually is if people are not to create hell on earth.

To bear a grudge, to continue a family quarrel for years and years, is a very effective way of poisoning our own soul (see Chapter 14) as well as those of the people around us, quite apart from its effect on the other party to the dispute. Some people have thick skins, and either don't get hurt terribly much by quarrels, or can recover quickly from wounds caused by harsh or careless words. Others, however, may lack such internal resources, with the result that even a relatively minor incident may gnaw away at them, and maybe even eventually destroy them.

The more culpable we think someone is, the harder we will find it to forgive them – it is likely to be easier to forgive someone who has caused the death of a loved one through careless driving than as the result of premeditated murder. Although we cannot wind the clock back, forgiveness does give us a way of undoing some of the damage that past wrongs have brought about, and is the *only* way we can escape the tyranny of the past, and prevent it from robbing us of the future. Forgiveness is important because otherwise we can become fossilised, trapped in the past like an insect in amber.

Tragedies can stop the clock, can freeze time in someone's life, or in the life of an entire family. There is the time-before-the-event, and the time-after, when things can 'never be the same again'. Forgiveness is about breaking the log-jam, about getting things moving, about starting the clock again. And this applies not only to victims, but also to perpetrators: until and unless there is self-acceptance (which is repentance) there can never be self-forgiveness; and without *that* there is no way of moving forward and escaping the power of the past to entrap and enslave in a downward spiral of self-hatred which gets expressed in a violent lashing-out at anyone and everyone within reach.

Forgiveness requires a measure of imagination in that it depends on a recognition that each of us operates within a causal nexus of inconceivable complexity. We choose to act, but our *freedom* to choose is circumscribed and constrained by our genetic endowment and our own personal history. The terrorism of September 11th grew out of a climate of despair and was nourished by religious fanaticism. To try and understand why people do terrible things is part of the process of learning to forgive them; not in the sense of belittling the enormity of their actions, but in the sense of seeing those actions as part of a wider picture, and therefore of relieving them of the entire burden of blame. This is a very delicate area, and there are bound to be those who object to what they see as an attempt to avoid anyone having to accept the responsibility that is rightly theirs. But the alternative is even less palatable: assuming that 'evil men' have no antecedents, and spring ready-formed from nowhere. To forgive is to acknowledge that we are all frail and fallible, that we all have *weaknesses*, that we are all *sinners*. It does not mean closing our eyes to horror, but being unwilling to cast the first stone.

Forgiveness may require time, and it will certainly involve effort – an effort of will. It requires us to refuse to be imprisoned by the past, and to want to reach out to the new life that is the future. Religious bigotry is alive and well in Northern Ireland, where the endless reliving of ancient battles and struggles enables the flames of old hatreds to burn with undimmed ferocity. Santayana noted that 'those who cannot remember the past are condemned to repeat it', mistakes and all; but it is equally true that those who won't let the past go are condemned never to live fully in the present.

For some people forgiveness may be impossible, and although in some cases such a reaction is completely understandable, it is nevertheless regrettable, because it condemns those involved to an endless round of hatred and bitterness. It is sometimes thought that closure may be achieved if a sufficiently extreme punishment is exacted on the guilty party, but this is probably a forlorn hope. Forgiveness and justice are both considered 'good things', but they may be mutually incompatible. Justice is about redressing imbalances by linking the past and the present, whilst forgiveness is about fresh starts and *writing off* past debts.

Despair can paralyse, whilst hope can energise. If we can see no way forward we may sink into lethargy and self-pity, but if a plan of campaign is produced we can throw ourselves into the project and draw upon hitherto-unknown wells of strength. This can certainly happen in the case of revenge, because it allows us to focus, not simply on being mad, but on getting even. Revenge is a completely natural and normal response, which is why Christianity is so unreasonable! Jesus wouldn't have anything to do with revenge, and demands (if we take him seriously) that we too turn our backs on it. Forgiveness is the opposite of revenge: it doesn't try to work out what punishment is appropriate, what someone 'deserves'. In fact it refuses to have anything to do with punishment at all, and instead looks at what is needed if some good is to be salvaged from what may be an unspeakably awful situation.

To the Christian, life is a gift from God; this means that life, *our* life, is contingent, accidental – it might not have been. For the fact that it *is*, that we *are*, we ought to be unceasingly grateful, and celebrate each new day as yet another free gift, *whatever it may bring*. To forgive is to embrace the realisation that nothing is ours by right, and whatever is taken from us we cannot demand or expect any form of restitution (which is what retributive punishment amounts to): 'freely ye have received, freely give'. (Matthew 10: 8) Those who have no sense of the gracious givenness of life will have no corresponding sense of reciprocity: if you don't think that you've received anything, you may not feel that giving (including *for*giving) is a normal part of being human. 'To give and not to count the cost' is an alien idea to many people, who view life instead as a sort of calculus, operating according to rules of strict fairness, where 'getting one's just deserts' is the central principle. Christianity offers a different picture, which can be commended both on religious grounds, and on the grounds that it offers a much better route to human flourishing. In fact, of course, these two grounds turn out to be identical, two ways of saying exactly the same thing.

The essence of forgiveness is **acceptance**, and this has to be unconditional: it can never be a case of 'forgiveness *if* '. Life's slings and arrows are *accepted* with a shrug, even those deliberately despatched by other people. And people's frailties and failings are also accepted with as much tenderness as we can muster. By trying to salvage something from the hopes and dreams that human wilfulness and cruelty have shattered, forgiveness aims to achieve some form of *redemption*. The traditional Christian view is that this is what Christ came to do, and if we follow his teachings on forgiveness we can ensure that he did not die in vain; that the new life he hoped to bring is realised in and through us, as we show that it really *is* possible to break free from the shackles of the past and start again: day after day after day.

Chapter 35

THINKING ABOUT LIFE AFTER DEATH

Our age is a curious mixture of the sceptical and the credulous. Some people find it difficult to take anything at face value, whilst many others find it difficult not to take *everything* like that. The result is that some find the claims of religion to be completely unfounded, whilst others have no real problem in accepting all that the Bible and the Church tell them. This is particularly the case with regards to life after death. For most people it's probably an attractive idea, but some find it preposterous whilst others find it perfectly plausible. No one *chooses* to believe or disbelieve anything: the position they occupy reflects how they happen to respond to the information they have, given the sort of person that they are. It would be as ludicrous to condemn someone who found the idea of life after death unproven, as it would be to congratulate someone else who saw it as self-evident.

The problem is that Christianity has become so identified with the ability to believe all sorts of peculiar things, that the more of these someone can manage, the more 'faithful' or 'religious' they may be thought to be. But scepticism and gullibility are each morally neutral, and the sooner attention is focused on the kind of life that people lead rather than the sort of religious thoughts that they have, the more attractive (and possible) Christianity will be to the thoughtful outsider.

It has often been said that without the prospect and promise of life after death, Christianity itself has no value: in other words, unless it provides a passport to eternity there's no point in bothering with it. Indeed, many would say, unless it goes on forever there's no point to life itself. But although these are common enough views, there's no reason to accept them. In fact, significant numbers of Christians have no belief in life after death, and this is so among an increasing number of regular church attenders.

As with so many articles of faith, life after death is something that many people can't get their minds around. Some see it as so ridiculous that it provides further reason for rejecting the whole of religion as simply pie-in-the-sky-when-you-die. But for many millions this vision has offered hope, which, given the awfulness of their everyday life, is something greatly needed. Marx famously called religion the opium of the people, and saw it as a tool of social and political control: so long as people's eyes can be kept fixed on the next life, there's less risk of them kicking up a stink about conditions in this one.

But however comforting or socially useful belief in life after death may be, the question remains as to whether the idea is well-founded. Many of the people who claim to believe in it don't tend to think too much about it, perhaps because the whole thing can begin to creak a bit as soon as it's looked at closely, in the same way that we might wonder whether an antique chair is capable of supporting our weight (better not try it!) All sorts of questions about life after death can be asked, such as: (i) After they die, do people have bodies, and if so what sort? ('spiritual bodies' aren't special sorts of bodies, but word-play) (ii) Are we reunited with our loved ones, and if so can we recognise them by their bodies? (what age of body?) (iii) Are there animals in 'the next life'? (iv) Does anything *happen* in eternity? (v) What it's like in heaven? (vi) What about hell? (rather less tends to be said about this, not least because most people feel that the subject will have little personal significance for them: as Sartre almost said, 'hell is for other people').

The open-minded sceptic would say that *not a single one* of these questions can be answered with any degree of confidence. She'd agree that there are plenty of *supposed* answers around, but they are entirely speculative – however confidently they may be stated! And when others point to various biblical passages and claim that they provide grounds for belief in life after death, she might respond that, quite apart from the impossibility of arriving at some 'correct interpretation' of such passages, there is the more basic problem of knowing what sort of *status* to accord them in the first place.

There is, of course, no necessary connection between religious belief and life after death. It's perfectly possible to believe in the existence of God *and* to anticipate extinction at death; just as it's perfectly possible to claim that there is no God, but to look forward to another life (or indeed lots of them) after this one. But perhaps the most important point is that in practical terms *life after death doesn't actually matter at all*, in the sense of affecting how we live each day. Some people have suggested that if there weren't the carrot-and-stick prospects of either eternal bliss or eternal punishment there would be no reason for people to behave decently. Quite apart from the fact that there is no evidence to support such a claim, this is a truly depressing view of human nature, implying that people are actually incapable of genuinely moral behaviour, which requires an attitude of selflessness and respect for others, completely unrelated to any benefit that may come our way. By definition, genuinely selfless behaviour *cannot* take account of what may or may not happen to us in a future life – which is why it can be argued that belief in life after death may actually make it impossible for someone to behave in a genuinely selfless, disinterested way.

Our imaginary sceptic would conclude that the evidence for our post-mortem existence is sketchy to say the least, and whether we continue to exist in some sense after death is something that only time will be able to tell. Dogmatism is (as always) unhelpful, and open-mindedness and humility (perhaps combined with a measure of hopeful anticipation) the only honest and intelligent attitude. Many people would find such a position highly unsatisfactory because its very open-endedness admits the possibility that death really could be the end. They might say that the reason why religion is so important is that it offers both certainty and hope. But is this what religion is about? And if so, is it what it *has* to be about?

It is undeniable that many of those who attend church feel the need for religious certainty, together with hope for their continued post-mortem existence. But it is also undeniable that such things count as *obstacles* to considerable numbers of those on the edge of the church, because they make Christianity seem like an exercise in wish fulfilment. About one-third of churchgoing Anglicans do not believe in life after death, together with some two-thirds of the population as a whole. Far from offering them a reason to take Christianity seriously, the idea of life after death reinforces in their minds the view that the whole thing is crazy.

This doesn't mean that Christianity, even Open Christianity, should somehow abandon the idea of life after death: it's far too important to far too many people for that. But it does mean that unless it is prepared to allow a variety of understandings of the idea, it is bound to continue to become ever more irrelevant to ever more people (see Chapter 9). One such approach focuses on life after the death of the self. It is the anticipation of our own disappearance that makes death such a fearful thing, but in fact the teachings of Jesus urge that we should be actively seeking this. To focus on the needs of others, to lose oneself in the present, to be so caught up in the business of living fully, is to escape from the tyranny of the self – and therefore from the fear of the *end* of the self.

If our imaginary sceptic feels about as confident as she can be that the present world is the only world, it means that life acquires an urgency and a preciousness. Death is only ever a heartbeat away, and this means taking with ultra seriousness the admonition by Marcus Aurelius to 'live each day as though one's last'. His main theme was the need to make the most of the everyday: 'when you arise in the morning, think of what a precious privilege it is to be alive – to breathe, to think, to enjoy, to love', and this can be done without any reference whatsoever to life after death. The very fragility of the wings of a butterfly is what constitutes their wonder, and the same might be said of human life. Those who think that this life is the only life may well feel a greater sense of responsibility to help create a world of justice and peace, a world in which people's feelings and needs are treated with total respect and seriousness.

There is a diversity of understandings within the Church about life after death. This variety needs to be recognised and celebrated, because it means that those on the outside are likely to be able to find church members who share their views, and who also find support from their faith. All too often Christianity has directed its gaze to the future rather than glorying in and trying to squeeze every drop of joy from the present. Whatever people's views on the subject of life after death, religion needs to be seen as a way of affirming the value of *this* life. When Jesus said that he had come 'to bring life in all its fullness' he presumably meant it: we need to live as if *we* mean it as well.

Chapter 36

THINKING ABOUT THE MEANING OF LIFE

What's the point of it all? Lots of people feel that unless life 'goes on' after death, nothing makes sense. Not only that, but the form in which it 'goes on' has to be similar to this life, so that they are able to reunite with loved ones, and never again feel the pain of being separated from them. Such feelings are widespread and very understandable: but why *should* things be like this? The universe may be very different from the way we would like it to be. There is no 'Law of Life' that says the truth about it must be something we find appealing. Might it not be the case that, in fact, life *doesn't* 'make sense'?

The orthodox Christian view is that it does 'make sense', that it does 'have meaning', for the very good reason that it is all part of God's plan. This plan encompasses both this life and the next one, and ensures that (eventually) justice *will* be done and that despite appearances, things aren't just random and meaningless. In other words, our guarantee of meaning lies with God, and with the eternal life that he/she has arranged. But where does that leave the sceptic, or the significant numbers of Christians who don't believe in life after death? (see Chapter 35). Are members of these groups nevertheless able to find meaning in life, or are they bound to see everything as pointless?

Religion is an exploration into what really matters, what is truly worthwhile; and then an attempt to centre one's life on it. The assumption behind all this is that a life focused on particular ideals or towards particular goals is more satisfying than one that simply drifts, because these are the things that give life 'meaning' or 'purpose'. But in our eagerness to grapple with the question as to whether religion is able to give meaning to life, it's easy to overlook altogether the prior question as to whether there can actually *be* such a thing as 'a meaning of life'.

One of the regular contributors to the 'Brains Trust' programmes of the 1940s was the philosopher Professor C.E.M. Joad, who would invariably begin his contribution to the discussion with the words '*it all depends what you mean by*' whatever it was. Probably many people found this (apparent) nit-picking rather irritating, and just the sort of thing a philosopher *would* say. But it needed to be said: and it *still* needs to be said! Before any question can be addressed it's vital that the terms are understood, and the more abstract and profound the question, the more important this is. All too often people use ethical or religious language in quite a casual way, as if they were simply talking about their shopping list or their furniture. And so if someone asks 'what is the meaning of life?', the first thing that needs to be said is 'it all depends what you *mean* by "the meaning of life"'.

Douglas Adams, in *The Hitch Hiker's Guide to the Galaxy* said that the meaning of life was forty-two. It isn't of course, and we can be completely certain that it isn't because a number *can't* be an answer to a question like that. What we can't be so certain of is knowing what *would* count as an answer. Many Christians say that the answer to life's questions is Jesus Christ: but as the spoof wayside pulpit notice has it, 'If Jesus is the answer – what is the question?' In other words, what does it *mean* to say that 'Jesus is the answer?' – the answer to *what*? Before something can *count* as an answer to a question, we've got to be able to say *why* it counts. A non-believer would be bound to ask, quite reasonably, what the expression 'Jesus is the answer' actually amounts to.

Questions usually aim to find out information: what time does the train leave? What is the boiling point of water? Who won the Cup in 1986? We know the sort of answer we're looking for, and so even if the information we're given is incorrect, it will at least make sense. But some questions are of a completely different order altogether. They're a way of expressing puzzlement, and 'what is the point/meaning of life?' is like this.

Most people, most of the time, wouldn't ask it: it tends to get asked only in moments of despair, when someone is wondering whether he's got the strength to carry on. It's obvious that there's something odd about the question, because there's no answer that can be given that would resolve it to everyone's satisfaction. If I want to know who won the Cup in 1986, and someone says it was Liverpool, then provided I believe them, the matter is at an end (even if the answer is wrong). But there's *nothing* that is guaranteed to achieve closure in response to a question about the Meaning of Life. It's not a case of perhaps not *believing* the answer someone might give: the problem is that the 'answer' to such a question can't be given by someone else, but has to be discovered by oneself.

So why bother to think about it at all? Because life is too precious to waste, and thinking about what it amounts to will get us to reflect on our most basic values, on our hopes and our dreams, on what really matters to us. We don't tend to ask philosophical questions for the sheer disinterested joy of it, and a question about the Meaning of Life is almost bound to be a personal, particular, existential question masquerading as a general one. What I'm *really* doing is expressing uncertainty about the direction that my life should take – and hoping that there's some formula, some blueprint, some *authority*, that will relieve me of the burden of having to take responsibility for my own choices and actions.

A lot of religion is like this, with people trying desperately to pass the buck for their own lives. The more responsibility that can be handed over in this way, the more people are attracted to it, with the fastest growing brands of religion being those that require the least thinking (and therefore the least measure of responsibility) on the part of their members. When someone asks what is the point of life, it may amount to a request to be shown one or more worthwhile projects that they would find satisfying and fulfilling. Because people differ, there cannot be just one kind of project that would do this for everyone, and so the search for a universally applicable 'point to life' is a nonsense.

Immortality is something that many people crave, not least because of the assumption that a life that goes on forever can have a 'meaning', whereas one that is terminated by death does not. The fear of the void, of eternal nothingness, is very real, and leads many people to wonder whether any of what they do or say matters if it all comes to an end. Those who think like this find it odd that they are surrounded by people also moving steadily towards death, but who still seem to find plenty of things to smile about. How can this be possible? Have they somehow managed to blot out the awful reality of it all, or have they found a way of dealing with it so that it doesn't have the power to overshadow everything?

There's no doubt that we fill our lives with ephemera and trivia; we become passionate about football matches or political scandals, we get deeply involved in DIY or gardening. These things give pleasure, although the author of the Book of Ecclesiastes felt that it all amounted to nothing. But does it? Even if it really does all come to an end, why should that somehow invalidate the pleasure felt? Is there not an intrinsic sanctity in each precious moment? Joseph Campbell commented that although 'people say that what we're all seeking is a meaning for life, I don't think that's what we're really seeking. I think that what we're seeking is an experience of being alive ... so that we actually feel the rapture of being alive'. We want each day to be joyful and fulfilling, so that when we go to bed, we are at peace with ourselves and the world.

Many people, tragically, never experience this, and spend their time in a mixture of turmoil and ennui. Not every problem has a solution, and it would be naïve to assume that religion offers some sort of simple resolution of their difficulties. In an age when people often try to shift the burden of responsibility on to others, it is only natural that the less reflective should think that all human problems (bereavement, divorce, unemployment, illness, depression and so on) can be ironed out, that everything can be made better. Tragedy, in all its forms, is part of the human condition, and it's only in the world of make-believe that it isn't.

Christianity focuses on the centrality of love and the awesomeness of life, and these are the things that can give satisfaction (and hence 'meaning'). The stories of Jesus show *self*-giving, *life*-giving love at work, and provide an example to try and follow. The self-centredness that is so characteristic of depression and other forms of mental illness illustrates why we have to look to the needs of others if we are to break free from the confining, paralysing power of the self. Treating other people with the dignity and respect that is their right is always going to be hard, which is why the teachings of Jesus have so little appeal in a society whose members tend to be concerned largely (in some cases almost exclusively) with themselves. Asking questions about the Meaning of Life, however, does at least raise the possibility that they might be encouraged to look outwards and upwards, which in itself makes the exercise worth doing. Such questions force us all to consider what really matters to us, what direction our life is taking, what our priorities are: things that are at the very heart of the religious quest.

Religion is all about the search for meaning, the search for fulfilment, the search for inner peace. Everyone with an ounce of reflection and sensitivity in them would agree that the search for these is at the heart of any worthwhile life. Some would say that genuinely satisfying answers can only be found in terms of our being part of God's plan, which encompasses both this world, and life after death, and ensures that, eventually, justice *will* be done and that despite appearances, things aren't random and meaningless. Others are able to find fulfilment without making such assumptions, as a result of living fully in the transient world of the here-and-now. Many people find this less satisfying because their focus is on the future, rather than the present. The implication of this is that the present moment (*any* 'present moment') is in itself of little or no value. But because the only place where we can *ever* live is in the present moment, if 'meaning' is to be found anywhere, it must be in the present.

Life can have 'meaning' or 'purpose' when people pursue goals that seem to them to be worthwhile. 'Purposeful' is the opposite of 'meaningless', and although someone who lived a totally aimless life could say that his life was purposeless, it would make no sense at all for someone whose life was focused on all sorts of interesting projects to say the same thing. This means that life *can* be worth living, that it *can* be 'meaningful', even *without* a belief in life after death: indeed, even without a belief in God.

Chapter 37

THINKING ABOUT QUANTUM THEOLOGY

The great physicist Niels Bohr once remarked that anybody who is not shocked by quantum theory has not understood it. Most people, of course, don't know the first thing about quantum theory, and far from being shocked by it are completely indifferent to it. It's the same with theology: most people don't know and don't care about the developments that have taken place over recent decades in the range of ways of thinking about God. And regrettable though this might seem, perhaps it's just as well, because the majority of them would probably feel upset and angry if they did know!

It's commonplace to bemoan the low levels of scientific literacy in our society, but levels of theological literacy are far lower. There's nothing surprising about this, in that all pupils have to attend science classes until they leave secondary school, whereas only a minority will have gone to *any* Sunday School lessons, and those who did are likely to have stopped before they left primary school. And just as people with only a very elementary understanding of physics will be unable to make much sense of cutting-edge physics, those with effectively *no* understanding whatsoever of theology will be at a complete and utter loss when faced with cutting-edge theology!

One of the great scandals of quantum physics was the idea that light could *either* be understood as a wave *or* as a series of particles: quite apart from the theoretical problems this raised, it clearly offended against basic common sense. At least as bad in this respect was the idea that it is possible to know *either* the momentum of a subatomic particle *or* its position, but not both. Initially, this was thought to be a problem of measurement, but it became clear that it was a problem of reality: particles such as electrons apparently *simply do not possess* both position and momentum simultaneously! Reality suddenly seemed a much stranger place than had been thought, and in important respects it stopped being possible to think of reality 'out there' as having some sort of independent existence: what is 'there' depends on who is doing the looking. The idea that reality can be *viewed* in very different ways, because it can *behave* in very different ways, is deeply unsettling. It means that the universe is an essentially indeterminate place, one that is far more mysterious than was once thought, and in fact one that we cannot, in any ultimate sense, fully *understand*.

The Newtonian world was a regular albeit complex place, but since the development of quantum theory, physics has lost its innocence. The story of the Garden of Eden shows how essential ignorance is for innocence, whilst that of the Tower of Babel illustrates how suspicious religion is to any attempt by people to gain some sort of control over their environment. The utterances of many religious leaders seem to suggest that ignorance is still essential to religion. But not only is this a counsel of despair to those within religion who value the use of intelligence; it also leads to many of those outside feeling that religion has nothing to offer them.

To the apparent dismay of large numbers of the faithful, theology has lost its innocence, in the same sort of way as physics. They may yearn for the equivalent of a no-nonsense, back-to-basics campaign in religion, which is the response of people in a time of crisis. During the Depression years of the 1930s, the economist J M Keynes commented that 'practical men, who believe themselves to be quite exempt from any intellectual influences, are usually the slaves of some defunct economist'. All our ideas come from somewhere; and that means from someone – and this includes what might be called the 'common-sense view' of religion. But just as developments in physics have shown the 'common-sense view' of the world to have severe limitations, new thinking in theology has shown the 'common-sense view' of religion to be far from the whole story – and maybe simply the musings of 'defunct theologians'.

The religious world has come to seem a much stranger place than many thought or feared, and just as very many physicists fought against the implications of quantum theory, many theologians (supported and cheered on by most of the clergy) have tried to resist the new religious thinking. Classical (Newtonian) physics continues to work well enough for most purposes, and it's only when the world is being studied at the atomic or sub-atomic levels that it breaks down. Similarly, the conventional thinking about God works well enough for most people most of the time, but there are those for whom it doesn't work at all, *any* of the time. These are the people who need an alternative framework, if they are to be able to do something with the idea of God.

One such radical framework is 'non realism', which suggests that God can be understood in a non-objective sense; not as a being who has some sort of existence independent of us, but as a way of summing up our ideals, and helping us to focus ourselves on those things we find to be of ultimate importance. Such an approach may be seen as threatening by those who hold a conventional ('Newtonian') view of God, but there is no good reason why they should think like that. It is not some sort of rival position that is being offered as a substitute ('*either* the traditional view *or* the non realist view: choose between them!') but as a complement to the traditional picture. However, as with quantum theory, the very *idea* that there may be very different ways of looking at something is unsettling to those who have a psychological need for the world to seem a simple and safe place.

Einstein, despite being a major figure in the development of quantum theory, argued passionately against the idea of indeterminacy (in his words, 'God does not play dice' with the universe).

In the same sort of way, many eminent theologians find the idea of non realism so offensive that they cannot entertain the notion of allowing it to exist alongside more conventional views. It might be that their main objection is an intellectual one, but it seems altogether more likely, given the level of their hostility, that it is something much deeper. Just as Einstein rebelled almost instinctively against the consequences of quantum theory, many conventional theologians find the implications of non realism so disturbing that they cannot bear to give it houseroom. In quantum physics the subject-object distinction came to seem much less firm than it had been, and non realism and other radical theologies offer a similarly fundamental shift in thinking, with their suggestion that God doesn't have to be thought of as 'out there', but might instead be thought of as being 'within'; as an integral part of each of us.

The widely held idea is that unless God is 'real' there can be no point to religion. By 'real' is meant something like 'exists independently', which means that unless God is somehow 'out there' religion is a waste of time. Unfortunately, however, there is no way of establishing the truth about the independent existence or otherwise of God, and therefore no way of distinguishing between what people *think* about God and what is the *truth* about God. All we've got, and all we can *ever* have, are people's views on the subject. Faith is commitment to a particular religious picture, and so one person's faith may involve seeing God in realist terms, whilst someone else may see God in non realist terms. The orthodox may feel that non realists are involved in some sort of deception, (maybe *self*-deception, as much as anything) and cannot, with integrity, be involved in religion. But non realists have shown that their religious life is likely to operate in exactly the same way as anyone else's: they pray, read the Bible, receive communion, and so on – and they do all these things in good faith and with a clear conscience!

Quantum theory, despite being a scandal and a source of bafflement to many, has been able to help physicists make sense of phenomena which otherwise would have eluded them. In the same way non realism, which is the religious equivalent, has shown itself capable of providing a picture that has helped some of the most intellectually acute critics of Christianity to take a full part in it. There is no way that it could (or should) displace the conventional picture, and no wish on the part of those who find it helpful to try and bring this about. Neither is there any likelihood that most of those for whom the conventional picture already works will be able to understand it at all. To them it will continue to seem a paradox, a scandal and an impossibility ('how *can* you worship a God who isn't there?').

In physics the new thinking has displaced the Newtonian picture, for the simple reason that most of the problems being addressed by physicists are in fields where quantum theory applies. This isn't true in theology, because most believers find the realist model perfectly satisfactory. Of course, there are far more people outside the churches than inside, but there is no way that most of the outsiders could ever be tempted to engage with religion via the ideas of non realism. These are (and will remain) very much a minority taste, of use only to a limited number. This is why there is no reason for anyone to be concerned that such views will infect the whole of Christianity. There is a far greater probability of religion in our society simply fading away than of non realism actually capturing the public imagination.

But despite all this, the quantum shift in theological thinking is something that is capable of reaching at least some of the people that other theological thinking cannot reach. If non realism helps them to become involved in the life of the Church, whose purpose is to transform lives and thus change the world, far from being the threat that some consider it to be, it can act as another strand in the attempt to create a more open and loving society. And that, after all, is the point of the whole exercise.

SUGGESTIONS FOR FURTHER READING

Adams, Jim	*So You Think You're Not Religious?*, Cowley Publications 1989
Adams, Jim	*So You Can't Stand Evangelism?*, Cowley Publications 1994
Boulton, David	*The Trouble with God*, John Hunt 2002
Byrne, James	*God - Thoughts in an Age of Uncertainty*, Continuum 2001
Cupitt, Don	*The Sea of Faith*, BBC 1984, SCM Press 2003
Cupitt, Don	*Reforming Christianity*, Polebridge Press 2001
Cupitt, Don	*Is Nothing Sacred?*, Fordham University Press 2002
Dawes, Hugh	*Freeing the Faith*, SPCK 1992
Freeman, Anthony	*God in Us*, SCM Press 1993, Imprint Academic 2001
Geering, Lloyd	*The World to Come*, Bridget Williams Books 1999
Geering, Loyd	*Christianity without God*, Bridget Williams Books 2002
Good, Jack	*The Dishonest Church*, Rising Star Press 2003
Hart, David	*Faith in Doubt*, Mowbray 1993
Holloway, Richard	*Godless Morality*, Canongate 1999
Holloway, Richard	*Doubts and Loves*, Canongate 2001
Hunt, John	*Daddy, Do You Believe in God?*, John Hunt 2001
Miles, Tim	*Speaking of God*, William Sessions 1998
Rees, Frank	*Wrestling with Doubt*, Liturgical Press 2001
Shaw, Graham	*God in our Hands*, SCM Press 1987
Spong, John	*Why Christianity Must Change or Die*, HarperCollins 1999
Spong, John	*A New Christianity For a New World*, HarperCollins 2001
Ward, Keith	*God - A Guide for the Perplexed*, Oneworld 2002
Webb, Val	*In Defense of Doubt*, Chalice Press 1995

The Sea of Faith network (www.sofn.org.uk) and *The Centre for Progressive Christianity* (www.tcpc.org) together with with its British branch (www.pcnbritain.org.uk) are excellent resources for Open Christians, and have lots of other references and links. The Radical Faith (www.radicalfaith.org) and Religion Online (www.religion-online.org) websites are also highly recommended.